Creating Digital Value For Members

The First Stop on the Road to Relevance for Non-profits and Associations.

Clive Roux

The goal of this book is to rewrite the non-profit manual for the 21st century. Providing a new set of tools, thinking and examples of where non-profits need to go in creating new value for members.

The underlying assumption of the book is that the non-profit executive must get involved personally in the shift to a user centric, design driven approach to member value creation. This is the problem-solving approach of all major successful brands. It integrates digital technology into the core of the non-profit's way of thinking.

Roll up your sleeves, write, code (a little bit), configure and tag. It is the only way that you will gain a real understanding of the potential of the new digital world for non-profits.

Author: Clive Roux
Editor: Cherer Defiori

Contents

Introduction

In the Digital age, non-profits find themselves less relevant than they were in the 20th century. This is not always obvious as most non-profits are doing OK since the recession of 2008 and therefore many non-profit leaders will question the need to change or take on the enormous (but exciting) work that this book outlines to gain digital relevance for members.

Assumption 1: It is understood that community now means virtual as well as physical.

LinkedIn, Facebook, Twitter, Google+, Instagram, Snapchat, Meet-up Groups, etc. No more needs to be said.

You now have real internet competition.

The case for change was laid out clearly in 2011 in **Race for Relevance** by Harrison Coerver and Mary Byers appealed to many non-profit executives because it struck a nerve. Yes! Things needed to change, and indeed keep on changing, but the authors did not describe what these "things" were.

What resonated was the feeling of being "less relevant in the digital age".

- There was new competition
- Current governance structures in place that made decision making slow.

The authors described the changed circumstances within which non-profits find themselves operating today accurately and made a strong case for the strategic changes needed in non-profit governance to become much more responsive and business led.

They correctly identified the need for non-profits to embrace digital technologies. They provided great advice and the first clues as to how to start moving in a new direction towards relevance.

What they did not describe was what relevance looked like. I suspect because the assumption was that it would be something different for all non-profits. However, like conferences or magazines work for most, I am sure that the underlying ideas in this book will as well.

Assumption 2: The focus of most content produced should be on the members, their firms, projects and thoughts. Not the non-profit structure, staff and programs!

Coerver and Byers advice to move Non-profits governance from slow moving to nimbler decision-making structures helps pave the way for bigger changes needed to become more relevant.

What they did not address were the changes needed in the value proposition and "product/service offer" of non-profits. This book tackles that aspect of the change needed.

They correctly identified that non-profits approach to technology had to change but did not elaborate on how it would need to change. Specifically, what new capabilities and competences would be needed to compete in a digital world. These are addressed in Chapter 4.

While they pointed out that products and services needed to be rationalized, the competences of Design, Product Management and development were not addressed as the enablers needed to achieve those changes.

Nor did they address the modern methodologies that are used to gain the insights about needed, targeted products and service solutions.

The creative competences needed to develop new products and services are a huge missing element of the modern non-profit as compared to their for-profit competitors.

It is no wonder then that more than 10 years on little real progress has been made on the road to relevance by most Non-profits.

My intention is for this is a follow up text to Race for Relevance with a specific focus on the "how to use"

How to use modern creation tools and techniques and how to use digital technology to create new value for members.

It assumes that you have read Race for Relevance and that you are now looking to build on the powerful ideas that you have implemented from that book.

Assumption 3: To fully participate in the digital age, you must be prepared to write and develop new code.

Whether you chose to buy that competence in or develop it in-house is your choice but understand that no great company has ever become great by buying in their core competence!

This book addresses the new mindset, competences and ways of working required to create new value using digital technology for non-profits.

My experience doing this for Philips Electronics and then running two non-profit's the past 10 years has enabled me to demonstrate that these ideas work for non-profits.

They are not the only ideas on the road to relevance, hence the subtitle, the first stop. However, they are clearly the start of non-profit business model 2.0. Hopefully I can illustrate the scope for new possibilities by adopting a digital mindset in sufficient detail for you to figure out how to create your own products and services using digital technology.

Thinking digital first unlocked a whole new direction in value creation for the non-profits I have run that did not exist before and that you still do not hear many talking about in articles about non-profit CEO's and issues. There appears to be a real lack of knowledge and understanding about the internet and its role in value creation.

My goal is to show you a door to a new world of digital opportunities for you to explore. It will also make your work more exciting as you work towards implementing these new ideas and empower you in a way that you have not felt before. Embracing digital can do this for you.

This book should deliver:

1. A framework for thinking about digital services creation
2. An understanding of the competences required
3. Some solutions that will make an immediate difference

4. Set you on a new course towards relevance using digital technology as your building blocks
5. Provide examples to get you to non-profit 2.0 level and delivering new value quickly

The example in this book applies specifically to a professional non-profit, but the principals apply to all non-profits.

When reading the book, consider that the outcomes and results used as illustrations apply to a professional non-profit, while the thinking, skills, tools and methodologies apply to all non-profits.

The illustration is one clear example of how the ideas and principles can be applied and is not intended to be the only way to apply them at all.

Chapter 1

The strategic argument.

Why do you need to focus on digital technology and building a creative competence within your organization?

The only reason to write a new strategic plan is because your circumstances have changed in some way and your old plan is no longer addressing the new, changed circumstances.

How have your circumstances changed since the early 90's?

- Non-profits have real for-profit competition to create communities, offer knowledge and education today
- The internet offers far cheaper ways to create and offer value.
- Members time is more stretched today than 15 years ago
- Technology allows you to do more with less, which means you go down the cost curve and up the quality curve. Non-profits have not done that, making them feel even further behind their for-profit competitors
- Expectations have skyrocketed with the advent of Google, Facebook, LinkedIn and others
- A lot is expected for free today

All Non-profits complain (rightly so) of having to do a lot with a little. Therefore, technology is the ideal solution for doing more with less for non-profits.

As always, a picture is better than a thousand words:

Non-profits are competing in the modern world with a level of digital technology that is the equivalent of a Walkman as compared to the iPhone level that for-profit corporations are developing and using to compete with.

For-profit corporations understand the internet as a business tool versus the non-profit understanding of a website as an electronic brochure or at best a content portal.

The non-profit way of working with websites is making use of only 10-20% of what web technology can offer a non-profit. Therefore, non-profits are losing relevance.

Start thinking about your non-profit website as a multipurpose platform capable of constantly allowing you to create and deliver new value or apps like an iPhone instead of a single purpose fixed device like a Walkman or your present website. To achieve that you must build a creative competence within your staff function.

The first reason to change your strategy and include digital as a core part of that strategy is that you must start taking advantage of the incredible power the web

11

offers you to create new and improved value for your members before a competitor does.

What really changed in the context within which non-profits operate since the mid 90's that requires a new strategic plan?

The internet. It changed everything.

It made it possible for multiple organizations and even individuals to start offering on-line what was pretty much the exclusive domain of professional non-profits through the 20th century. Education, Networking, Inspiration and Information about a certain profession could all be offered easily and at much lower cost or as is most often the case, usually for free in the new content driven business model world of the internet, to your members via internet services. What's more the technology to build these services are widely available.

Most Non-profits did not embrace the internet early as they perceived that their competitive advantage was in physical and that the internet was somehow the opposite, or maybe even a threat and so withdrew further into their safe place.

Non-profits advantage is and must remain in physical, but the fact that the web exists and is open to anyone to use and is used by everyone means you have a responsibility to use the web to get a lot more efficient at what you do, offer much more value than you did before and invent new as-of-yet unheard of benefits for your members.

Even more significantly, because of the extremely low cost of entry to learn, use and modify digital coding, the internet has created a tool that all organizations are using to improve efficiencies by creating lighting quick connections by reducing obstacles and friction and delivering value globally in an instant.

If you are not scared by that, you should be, because these are the things that gnawed away at your relevance and at which you are now going to have to work hard at to get your relevance back again.

The real Unique Selling Proposition (USP) of a non-profit is still that they offer physical networking and physical interactions. They are still worth a lot. But many people connect virtually today and find it as fruitful if not more so as well as getting education via YouTube, Vimeo, their information free from Google, Wikipedia and many other sources.

Non-profits should never lose their edge in physical networking, BUT they can add the same amount of value to membership digitally, thus doubling their value to members as compared to today.

The speed with which the internet can deliver things to you means the amount of time people have or are prepared to put into a non-profit has changed. If your only advantage is your physical events and knowing that only a small percentage of your members attend them, you can see why your relevance has been suffering.

Today there are so many more options to occupy peoples time, that everyone feels more time starved. This is borne out by research. Solutions that require less of a time commitment than physical engagements such as conferences, workshops, meetings and education sessions are all rising in priority for professionals.

Non-profits went from having practically no competition to having multiple sources of competition (as did all other physical businesses) and we were not ready with our lumbering governance structures for the speed at which companies were forced to make decisions and change. In that respect Coerver and Byers were correct.

A good starting point for a strategy statement would be to consider delivering 50% of a Non-profits value physically and 50% digitally.

That is not as hard as it sounds. In fact, before you know it, you might be delivering 80% of your value digitally, at least to the 80% of your non-profit who are not involved like the top 10-20% are in networking and physically! Imagine delivering value to 80% of your members instead of 20%?

If you really want to become relevant to the profession, why not set your strategy to become:

A vital tool for the profession, one that they can't do as well in their careers or businesses without!

It's time to start thinking bigger about what Non-profits offer members!

Just think what has come at Non-profits in the last 20 years.

Alibaba started in 1999. LinkedIn started in 2004. Facebook got going in 2004, but only really became widely used in September 2006. Twitter started in 2006. The iPhone launched in 2007. In 2015 mobile access (53%) through smart phones and tablets overtook access through desktop computers.

These entities eventually started to look a lot like the networking, information, education and inspiration activities of non-profits, but at low cost, global scale and available on the go wherever you are. Never mind the millions of blogs, Meet-up groups and sharing economy offers such as Uber, Airbnb, Lyft etc. that have got going since then.

The business model for access to information has shifted dramatically from pay for access to a sponsored content/advertising model where access is free for all.

To access that advertising revenue stream, you need scale or an audience. For most advertisers looking at on-line promotion now days, Non-profits membership size really is not very interesting compared to their reach through other platforms on the internet. Many business verticals have struggled with this issue and many are only just starting to struggle with it now! Think how Uber and Airbnb are disrupting industries today. The so-called sharing economy is just getting going and they are powered by social media platforms and search!

Most non-profits have not been able to move their thinking about their websites much beyond the early 2000's idea of a website as an electronic brochure for the organization with some of the traditional back-end bits such as job banks, membership directories and non-profit management systems (AMS) tacked on.

The technologies and options have become a lot more favorable to think about digital technologies for non-profits in a very different way. This book will help you see the broader potential the internet offers a non-profit.

Partially, this is the case because most non-profit skills tend to be administrative, not creative, innovation and product/service development type skills.

This is one of the main reasons' non-profits are lagging far behind commercial organizations in terms of generating new value for their members or "customers" and even further behind in terms of understanding how to use digital technologies i.e. the internet/code/data/web search and marketing to create value cost effectively for a time starved audience.

Given the existence of the Internet and a world rapidly morphing from physical products towards code to do many of the same things far more efficiently, non-profits have absolutely no alternative! They must start to build their own creation competences in house and get on the digital value creation bandwagon in order to regain their relevance.

This book is about a new way of thinking about digital value creation in the context of a non-profit. It's about the tools and methodologies that will help you think about and design solutions for your member's problems and it will help you shift your competitive bar much higher digitally.

It will also give you some first ideas about the kinds of value you can generate for your members digitally to improve the non-profit value proposition and become more relevant again!

I use a single example, one I created internally with my team. I don't pretend that it is a great site or that it is the best site by any means, but I use it because of how effective it has been. A full description of the site is given in the last chapter with instructions of how to copy it so that you start on the foundations of 4 years' work and build from there.

This is a short book and a quick read, because our knowledge of creating new value is still slim. Hopefully you will learn from it and can add to that base of knowledge for all who live to do good in the non-profits.

Once you take the plunge, get a core creative activity going and start to play with code, design and user research, you will find you are having so much more fun that there is no way you will want to go back to where you are today, essentially maintaining a 40 year old non-profit status quo.

It won't take you long to figure out just how much more proactive you can become at value creation and your board and members will thank you.

Read quickly. Don't be afraid to spend lots of time experimenting and learning. Join the community of non-profit executives working on developing non-profit 2.0 (cliveroux.com/non-profit 2) and continue doing the great work you are deservedly known for!

Does your non-profit HQ look like this? It's typical of creative studios and internet startups. Imagine this as your new tightly packed fun filled open office! Break down the walls, pack 'em in, shorten the lines of communication and encourage more collaborative working and shared

17

information! This is also the first place where you can find the money to finance your new digital expansion!

Why do we assume that internet starts ups should be the only ones to have cool work environments, exciting work lives and be the ones who use digital technologies to create new value?

That is just crazy. All the tools, methods and technology are open for everyone to use!

It's time to step up and have some fun yourself!

Chapter 2

Understanding the internet

How does the internet differ from print media and non-profits?

The internet presents a huge opportunity for non-profits to develop new value/services!

The internet does three things well.

- Commerce transactions – cutting out the middleman
- Data - recording/delivering/sorting/filtering data
- Connecting - people, places, firms, interests, etc.

It does these far more efficiently than ever possible before at speeds not imaginable. In other words, its main advantage is to remove friction from these systems. A frictionless system operates at speeds that mean you have to think differently.

Most non-profit websites are closer to on-line brochures conceptually than full blown services like Google, Facebook or LinkedIn. They still operate pretty much like traditional print versus true digital services.

The three phases of development of a non-profit's digital presence.

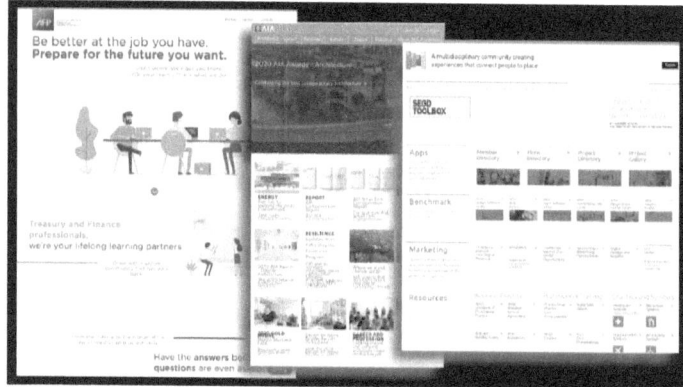

When it comes to creating an internet or digital strategy, non-profits to think about the development of their website in three distinct phases. This helps when describing the structures, competences and activities you will need to undertake to succeed in each phase, but as with most reality versus theory, the real-life process is less likely to be this clear cut as the three phases will tend to overlap each other.

Phase 1: Website as Digital Non-Profit Brochure (many associations are now past this)

a. The focus is on the non-profit as an entity; most content is dedicated to explaining who the non-profit is, what they do and why you should join it. 80-90% of non-profit websites are of this type still. When there are awards, they are generally listed rather than illustrated articles.

b. The structure is likely an html page structure or a simple Content Management System (CMS) implementation.
c. The site is likely built by an outside web development firm and the internal competences are limited to simple editing and or HTML manipulations
d. Internally there is probably one staff member responsible for the website who does all or most of the work on updating it. It is likely that updates are few and far between, except for weekly or monthly news.

Phase 2: Website as Content Portal

a. The decision to shift a website from an on-line brochure to a content portal is a first recognition that a website can do a lot more for you than acting only as an on-line brochure. That was where websites were in the 90's and early 2000's.
b. When shifting to become a content portal you can take one of two directions.
   i. Shift your entire focus from you to them! In the on-line brochure model the focus is non-profit, the entity first. In the content portal model think about the "non-profit" not as the staff and structures, **but rather as the members, their firms, projects and thinking about the profession and its development.**
   ii. Keep the focus on you, the non-profit and offer interesting content that enriches your members/visitors but loose the advantage of shifting the attention to your members! In the authors opinion, this is the most important single decision you need to make when determining

your digital strategy and it has the most far reaching effect on the value you can add. Be bold and shift the focus from you to them and you will not regret it.

iii. **The rest of this book is presented on the basis that you make this crucial decision!**

Phase 3: Website as Solutions Platform (a set of tools) for value delivery

a. The shift from a content portal to a platform comes when you start to ask what your members need information for? Websites are repositories of information and code to manipulate that information.

iv. What problems can your data and content help members solve?

v. How can your data and content help promote your member's profession?

vi. What data and content do they need to do their jobs better, benchmark more easily, set goals or targets with? Can your non-profit be a toolbox they use every day to make their jobs easier/more efficient/more fruitful?

vii. How can you connect them to potential clients visiting your website?

viii. How can you help them find employees to hire?

ix. How can you create useful discussions among professionals for learning or helping each other solve problems?

x. How can you educate clients, help raise expectations about levels of service, etc.

b. As you shift from a content portal to a Solutions Platform, so the need to become user centered becomes a vital part of the mindset shift you must undergo because there is nothing worse than creating a huge amount of work for your staff that will result in little added value for the membership! It is only by understanding member's workflows, daily problems and issues that you will be able to successfully build solutions to their actual needs.

There is a fourth phase rapidly developing around AI, marketing automation, customization and learning. That is the topic of a different book and is not dealt with here.

Versus other types of organizations, non-profits have made the least progress with understanding the possibilities that the internet can offer them to improve benefits and services for their members. They also have the least developed view of how to integrate the internet into their businesses and become innovators by using data and the internet to create new value for members.

In short while the vast majority of commercial organizations have been integrating the internet into their business value creation activities, non-profits have remained stuck in the physical world of networking and face to face interactions and while they to this better than anyone else, the changes in demographics, activities people are prepared to devote time to and the sheer number of platforms we all participate in have all taken a huge chunk of time away from the free time members have to devote physically to an non-profit now days. The only answer is to provide ways for them to economically and efficiently engage with you. On-line!

Why have non-profits fallen behind?

Until the mid-90's at least, most non-profits operated without competition. A lack of competition is never a good scenario to innovate in! Secondly non-profit professionals have a deep lack of understanding of how the Internet works and what it can do for them. For the most part non-profit professionals have been using the internet as a digital brochure with some legacy non-profit management functions tacked on. Therefore, they have not been making use of the most powerful business value creation tool to come along in the last 100 years to grow the value they provide to their members in the same way as for-profits have been doing.

It's time to correct that for non-profits by starting with an understanding of the differences between the physical ways and internet ways of doing things.

Characteristics of the internet.

Internet Characteristic 1: It does not care about you.

Like most of us, you believe that you live in a corner of the world where your members care about you (often lovingly because they pay to belong) and you assume, know or hope that the broader profession does as well. The Internet connects things together, but it does not care about you or your existence at all. It does not understand you, does not want to and has no use for you! If you want to be found on the internet, it is all up to you! Competing on the Internet really is about understanding how it works and using that to create a flow of traffic towards your website. Therefore, if you do not figure out how this jungle works fast, you will probably become the low hanging fruit that gets eaten first for breakfast! It will really help if you can get a strong competitive mindset about your web activities.

Which one of these connected bubbles are you? How does anyone find you? Without search finding your content is like searching for a needle in a haystack. Search is really important.

[http://intbio.ncl.ac.uk/?people=dr-katherine-james]

Internet Characteristic 2: It is more efficient than traditional technologies for running businesses, creating value and communication.

One of the most powerful benefits of the internet is that it removes barriers to access, removes friction that slows things down and does things very cost effectively using bytes rather than atoms. It also usually provides benefits to additional users at no incremental cost meaning it can easily scale. That is not the case for every magazine you print, or every seat you must provide at a conference or trade show which have real incremental costs associated with them.

On the internet, it is easy to enable and add additional benefits at a very small incremental cost versus any other technology.

The Internet is live 24/7/365. That means it works three times the number of hours a day that your staff do. Physically the non-profit is open 1827 hours a year as opposed to your website which is open 8,736 hours! That provides a huge opportunity for efficiency.

One of the simplest, yet most effective benefits of the internet is that it can enable all your staff to get access to the information they need to make better decisions and work from anywhere at any time.

Internet Characteristic 3: It is not one thing.

It is not a singularity. It is a mainly open platform that is infinitely variable and customizable to fit your needs. Imagine that.

Think about the Internet like a factory where all the raw materials you need exist and all the tools you might need to create something exists. All you need now is a plan of what you want and to build your ideal solution to your user's problems. Nothing could be simpler, right?

Internet Characteristic 4: It is BIG!

New Data Created on the Internet every minute:

EMAILS | 204,000,000
YOUTUBE | 72 HOURS NEW VIDEO
TWEETS | 277,000
PINTEREST PINS | 3,472
GOOGLE SEARCHES | 4,000,000
NEW WEBSITES | 380
BLOG POSTS | 1400
INSTAGRAM PHOTOS | 216,000
PANDORA | 61,141 HOURS OF MUSIC
APPLE APP DOWNLOADS | 48,000
FACEBOOK SHARES | 2,460,000

It is very, very BIG! Much bigger than any tool you have ever had the opportunity to use as a non-profit before. And what's more, it is the same as Apple, Google, Facebook and the other giants of our time are using. They have just figured it out faster and have applied a lot more resources, especially the creative resources to figuring out how to use it to answer user needs better. Now it is your turn.

Collaboration is the name of the game, building knowledge on top of paths others have formed, ideas others have found worked. There are hundreds of groups on the internet all collaborating to build value faster and at lower cost to all. You have to participate otherwise you will not be able to move fast enough or afford to stay in the race.

Internet Characteristic 5: The internet is mainly free

For the most part access to information on the Internet now days is mainly free. Information or content is the thing that interests people to come to your site in the first place. Search provides the mechanism for them to find that information or content. This is of course in direct conflict with the membership model of most professional/industry Non-profits. This characteristic will need very careful consideration as to the strategy that will help you survive and thrive under those conditions.

In addition to free access to information, access to code is also free for some pretty powerful tools that will give you a great big coding toolbox. To build the kind of digital tools for your membership that we illustrate in this book we recommend using Drupal instead of Wordpress because it has far more flexibility for you to manipulate it from the front end than Wordpress does and it is more suitable for complex websites with a lot of information as most non-profit websites contain. The learning curve to get started is steeper than

Wordpress, but it pays back handsomely when you want to customize your site later.

Drupal powers 3% of the websites on the internet and 15% of the top 10,000 sites. There are over 1,500,00 Drupal websites which means there is support and functionality for most things you can think of already available on the Drupal platform for you to download to start your customization with for free. Drupal is already incredibly popular with governments, education, non-profits and large enterprises.

Internet Characteristic 6: It flows like water.

Because it is mainly free, traffic on the Internet follows the flow principle going where it is easiest, where it finds the least resistance and roadblocks and simplest solution to visitor's problems. It does not care about the past, about heritage, experience, present scale or structures. It is a living organism meant to destroy complexity and inefficiency in the name of faster, easier and cheaper access to information and community. This is its sole reason to exist. The benefit is that he who provides solutions that meet those criteria wins against all incumbents regardless of resources, scale or heritage! And for that reason, it is redefining the rules of your engagement with the world whether you like it or not. This is the nature of your competition today.

The internet is rapidly evolving and reaching higher levels of intelligence and usefulness. It is moving from digital brochures to portals of content to social interactions to ecosystems of functionality that replace physical alternatives at a rapid rate. Whole new sets of tools to replicate and improve on physical functions keep appearing every year now and it can be very difficult to keep up but keep up you must.

Internet Characteristic 7: Pull, not push.

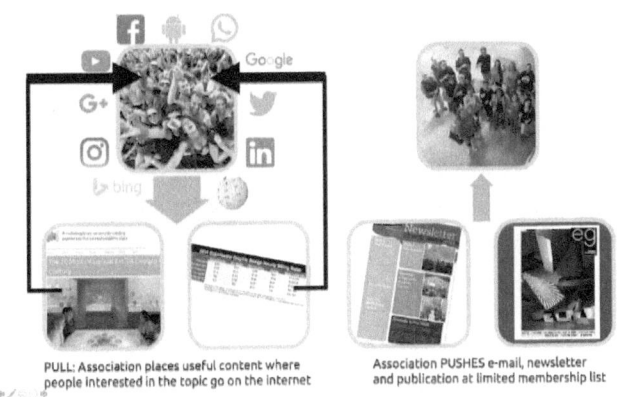

PULL: Association places useful content where people interested in the topic go on the internet

Association PUSHES e-mail, newsletter and publication at limited membership list

You don't want to have a website that feels like pushing water up a hill! The most important principle for most Non-profits to understand about the Internet is that it works on pull as opposed to your print, e-mail or other marketing devices that work on you pushing them out to a distribution list. You must create the flow effect. With the Internet, the clear majority of your traffic will come from how effectively you can pull the billions of people connected to the internet towards you. Content will play a huge role in helping you achieve that. That happens in several ways: **Search**, organic mainly, though paid could also be a strategy and **word of mouth** (mainly through social media) and placement or distribution. By far the most effective of these strategies is search, which for most websites' accounts for about 50-80% of their traffic.

The fact that the Internet works in exactly the opposite way to how you have been operating for 100 years is worth pondering for a bit. It is a huge fundamental shift in how you need to start thinking about your website/digital strategy.

The assumption (sometimes tested, but only very anecdotally) about your print magazine for instance is that about 5-10 people read each magazine a non-profit puts out. This grossly over inflates the supposed value of the magazine. The assumption is that by pushing the magazine into our members' offices, the information would be seen. Before pulling the plug on our award-winning magazine, I asked my board who had read the latest edition that had been (assumed to be) on their desks for about 2 weeks. Not one hand went up. Case closed.

Contrast that with our Google Analytics which told me with certainty, not anecdotally, that over 1,500 people a day were accessing and reading an average of 5 pages a visit on our website.

Every day!

SEGD is a small non-profit of only 2,300 members. Over 99% of those accessing our website are not members. That's good and bad news that we will come back to later. The point here though is that pull marketing and easy flow works infinitely better than push and at a fraction of the cost.

Internet Characteristic 8: Everything is measured and measurable!

This is a huge difference between the internet and print. On the Internet everything that happens is actually measured! This is good and bad. Good because you know what is going on. Bad because there is less going on than many would suppose by making broad sweeping assumptions as with a magazine!

Measurements on the web are probably not going to meet your expectations or assumptions! Therefore, it is worth becoming aware of and understand what average metrics look like on the webs to that you have a way of benchmarking your own websites performance.

Some of the easiest to reference numbers

- Average time on your site/pages. The average webpage visit lasts less than a minute. The average website visitor leaves a webpage in 10-20 seconds. If they stay longer than 10 seconds, they are more likely to stay on your site for longer. If they stay on a page for more than 30 seconds, the drop off rate will become flat. 30 seconds is a good time to aim for, but rather difficult to achieve as an average, so you may want to look for those visitors that you really do want to attract, i.e. potential members to ensure that they are staying for 30 seconds or longer. If you are search optimizing correctly, there will be a lot of visitors who do not know who you are, or what your members do and have found you through a search link. For them a much lower time between 10-15 seconds may already be a good goal to aim for, enough time to peak their interest and hopefully keep them on your site long enough to create a strong positive impression and perhaps encouragement to come back and investigate your profession again. (Reference: Microsoft Study)

- Average number of page read per visit. Another good indicator of engagement. 2.8 pages represent the average number of pages read on a site, it you are getting more than that you are on the right track. There are lots of content strategies that can be used to improve the number of pages read, some of dubious value such as dividing up articles, while other genuine tactics can really help to keep your members engaged such as links to the member's bio or firm to learn more.

- Other good metrics are number of pages read, number of visitors, new versus returning visitors and bounce rates. These are all basic measurements that will give you a quick picture of how you are doing. There are many more that you can customize or look for depending on what you are trying to measure.

Internet Characteristic 9: Robots control it. Seriously!

It matters not what your mother tongue is, you are going to have to learn "robot" or code in order to thrive on the internet and just like taking a trip to a foreign country, you are going to enjoy it much more if you can speak at least a few words in the language of your new host! They will appreciate you much more as well.

What is the most important robot that you need to get to know?

Search Engine Optimization (SEO) or the webs equivalent to physical mailing list print distribution will be one of your most important tools on the Internet, just as your mailing list is today. Search is the interface between you and your visitors and an understanding of search robots and the mechanics of search optimization for those robots (or filters as an easier way to understand them) will enable you to open a line of communication between you and the robots and for you to start to think in the way that the robot does so that you can get the robot to do what you need it to do for you. This particularly helpful robot type is referred to as a search crawler.

Don't underestimate the importance of SEO! Or the complexity of it for the mechanics are simple to grasp and learn but winning at search requires you to raise your game to the level of art!

As you grapple with Search Engine Optimization, you will discover along the way that you are now producing content for two very different audiences or target groups, search bots, the robots we are talking about here and humans, the target group you would like to read your content. Writing for search and human readers, combining this in a single piece of content is the thing that is going to lift you up from being a mechanic to becoming an artist.

Internet Characteristic 10: It extends your reach

The number of people who visit your website and who potentially could visit it are orders of magnitude greater than the size of the non-profit's membership. That means you have a reach that is far greater than you could afford with any print communications. What could you do with that reach?

What does your non-profit website do? Does it do anything that you could not do physically? Does it do anything different than your physical programs or does it just support them? Does it do anything more efficiently than you did physically before the internet? Do you have a clear Digital Strategy that defines what and how it should perform?

How much is it aligned with the ten principles above?

There is a saying that there is an App for everything! Is that true for your non-profit? Because that is what a non-profits website should be for members.

The above list are the principles of the internet needed to understand why the world around your non-profit is changing, the next set of characteristics or components describe the things needed to succeed at making value for non-profit members on the internet.

The components of a digital presence

Your presence on the internet is made up of several components. Each is like a tool that will enable you to create value for members by using them in different combinations to solve user problems. The key is you must understand what user problem you are trying to understand in order to know which tool to apply to fix that problem!

Think about these components as tools in your non-profit's digital toolbox:

1. Website Traffic - Visitors
2. Users and use cases/personas
3. Search
4. Usability/experience
5. Content
6. Tagging/Filters/Taxonomies and Indexes
7. Links
8. Data
9. Functions - Apps/modules
10. Configurations/Site Building
11. Code
12. Analytics
13. Digital Marketing
14. Brand
    a. Brand Values
    b. Visual Identity

Website Traffic - Visitors

Visitors are the people who discover your content or search terms and come to your site. In much smaller numbers, they are people who know who you are and type in your URL directly or come to you via social media platforms. If you are the number 1 term in a Google search, then the search traffic represents about 1-3% of the people interested in that term. Not a big percentage, which means there is still a lot more potential to explore out there. I.e. the number one position is definitely not the holy grail. Being on the first page is already a very good position to be in. Site visitors are interested in the content that you have, but not necessarily interested in you or your non-profit yet. At this point you have the chance to offer them something interesting that might persuade them that you are valuable enough to return to. If you achieved that, it's a good first step with first time visitors. Repeat visits indicate that you have something useful to offer.

Users and Use Cases/Personas

Most members make the mistake of thinking that the only people who visit the Non-profit's website are the members. This is especially true for the assumptions of members. That is the basic (incorrect) assumption that you will have to overcome with your community and quite possibly also your board. Taking SEGD as an example the number of members is only 0.3% of the UNIQUE visitors on the site every year!

What is clear is that there are many, many more users of the content than there are members of the non-profit. This is great news for members and their businesses. But if you view this in non-profit 1.0 terms it seems grossly unfair that 0,3% of the users are paying for the benefit that 99.993% of the users are receiving! Hopefully the staggering difference in the numbers will help you give up your notion of how things work and open your mind to rethinking exactly what it is you are doing with your non-profit, why you are doing it and for whom you are really doing it.

From the value creation point of view, it means that we have to be thinking about multiple audiences, not just the members. That is the old-fashioned way to see the web as simply a device to inform the members of what is going on. You will need a greatly expanded view of who the website is serving in order to create new value for a range from one-time visitors to regular users. Think members, the broader community of your profession/industry who are not members, the customers of your members and community, other people interested in the topic. I am quite sure you do not want to find yourself in front of your board explaining why you built your new website for 0.3% of its visitors and ignored 99.7% of them. The 99.7% could potentially provide client work, revenue and added acceptance or recognition of the great work your members do! In other words you need to think:

If ever there was a great reason to rethink your non-profit. This is it. You are designed to serve only 0.0007% of those interested in what your non-profit does! That is just flat our crazy.

What to do with this new realization?

The most fundamental questions to ask about this insight is,

How might you best create value FOR YOUR MEMBERS from the 99.7% of your website's visitors?

The overall goal will be to see how you can move those just vaguely interested in your content towards a higher engagement with your organization and your members. Questions such as these might help to get you thinking differently:

How might you move a casual visitor into a more regular visitor?

How might you move a regular visitor into an engaged visitor who cares for the topic?

How might you move an engaged visitor to become a member of the community?

How might you move a member of the community to become a member of your non-profit?

How might you move non-profit members from being passive to becoming more actively involved members?

Traffic and visitors are gold, or at least they can be turned into gold. Just ask Google, Facebook, LinkedIn, Twitter, or any other modern web driven company. These are all organizations whose role is to help people, network, connect, learn and become informed! Sound familiar? Anyone think LinkedIn is not a competitor of every professional non-profit?

Search

The (free) Internet works on PULL not PUSH! Search is the main mechanism for pulling or attracting viewers to your content from the internet. This very different to print where you "push" your content to people by physically distributing your magazine to them. E-mail is a digital push distribution. A website is a digital pull distribution. You should expect to gain about 50-80% of your traffic from search if you use the right CMS and set your website up correctly and optimize your content for search. Learning how to do search well is definitely a worthwhile skill to invest in as a non-profit, because of course you can choose to use the internet in a push mode by buying search terms through Google Adwords, or buying advertising, but that is completely unnecessary.

How does Search work?

Google (mainly) and other search engines have robot "crawlers" called search bots that visit every site on the web, indexing what words and terms exist on each site. They register whether the words appear in the URL, the title and their density (number of times) in the text amongst other things. Then using complex algorithms, they compare your page with similar pages from other sites, taking into account the traffic that each page on the sites receives, the links to those pages and a number of other factors including the links and retweets, likes etc. on social media. This is how they prioritize your content on a ranking of its relevance to viewers. Remember the algorithm is not "reading English", just scanning for repetition of words and terms, for mechanical things like the amount of people reading the page, how it appears in your code, how clear your websites code structure is, how it is linked to by other sites, indicating whether or not people see this page as a reference worth considering etc. It is a very complex, ever changing algorithm that is secret to Google and so therefore partially an art of backwards engineering for the rest of us, but you can get a long way by just following the basics.

This is roughly speaking how the robots decide whose page will occur first, second third etc. The top link receives the biggest traffic, but increasingly the large sites like Wiki, Facebook, Twitter, LinkedIn and others sit at the top and so people are scanning down the page to look for links they might find more relevant. People are starting to understand that they might need to look for sites in the search that they will recognize as more relevant to them. Registering on the first page of search should be your goal, not necessarily registering as the number one link that might be all but impossible for a small non-profit to achieve. SEO or Search Engine Optimization is a mechanical process as well as an art. Start with the mechanics which only requires you to follow a simple set of rules. You'd be surprised just how much additional search traffic that will bring you. For widely used terms though, you will need to employ the art, the art of writing compelling, interesting content that others would want to read and forward on to their friends.

Note: the toughest part of Search is getting an print oriented editorial staff to understand how they need to shift their thinking from how they have been writing for a magazine for instance and start to write for search in order to ensure that they meet the simple mechanical rules of search. Don't underestimate how big an effect this will have on the success of your search strategies. Check it often to gauge progress and stimulate or enforce search optimization rules as equal to grammar and editorial preferences because your editorial staff have in some ways also become your marketing or "distribution" staff! This is most likely not something they will appreciate or take to easily.

Usability/Experience

Usability is key now days. We are far past the point where bad user experiences in experimental sites is acceptable. The state of web design has moved far past learner stage with the advent of Content Management systems which help to guide and determine a lot of the usability of websites today, bringing the majority up to a reasonable standard at least.

How easily can a user get to the information they need?

Here are the top 10 web usability issues to avoid from the renowned Nielsen Norman Group.

1. Unexpected locations for content – people can't use content they can't find. Locations need to be based on the user's mental models of how content should be sorted, not the Non-profit's!
2. Competing links and categories – Category and link names need to make sense on their own, but also in Conjunction with other options on the site
3. Islands of information – information should not be scattered around the site in islands with no connections between them. Use related links to help users navigate between content that is hard to group in the same place.
4. Repetitive Links. It is not the quantity of the links it takes to get to information that counts, it is the quality of the links! Users should feel that they are getting closer to the information the more they click.

5. Hidden fees and prices. People want to know about process, subscription fees, postage and what is included before or at the beginning of the process.
6. Stranding users on Microsite. If you have to build a separate site and it is worth thinking 4 times about doing that, there needs to be easy ways for people to get back to your main site.
7. Poor search results. Site search is still a major weakness for many websites. People expect google quality results. Good luck!
8. Flawed filers and facets. Facets and filters generally improve user experience. However, they need to support real user needs.
9. Overwhelming users with information. Remember that readers generally scan, not read on-line!
10. Hidden Links. Users ignore ads. Avoid adding design to links that then look more like ads and are less seen by users.

Content

Content can be produced from data, from interviews, by writers and posters of blog content from your community, forums and chapter volunteers. There are many, many sources of content, but aggregating the content for your field is one way that you can add value to your profession and doing this digitally does not cost you more incrementally as compared to adding pages to a magazine or newsletter.

Digital publishing has the added advantage that it is easily accessible and available for anyone or a limited set of people to consume which provides options for you to decide how you want to share it and add value from it.

Good content draws an audience to your website. Great content is one of the cornerstones of creating value on the internet.

If you follow the route of creating digital value, you will definitely be creating a lot more content than you are today and that will be good for your position and relevance as well as for the profession.

Tagging/Filters/Taxonomies and Indexes

Originally websites were built using HTML. This was a language to position data or content such as images and text on a web page. The content was fixed per page, as if it was printed. Modern content management systems give you the ability to place content dynamically on a page using a variety of filtering techniques.

Pages don't exist as static entities anymore, but rather as code that contains rules to filter and fetch data from a database and present them on a screen in a preformatted way per a set of code called a CMS. This means that you can chose to filter and serve the same set of data in a variety of different ways. Tags (labels in a library), vocabularies (collections of tags for instance city names) and indexes formed using the tags or vocabularies are one of the main mechanisms used to filter the content or display it in different groupings.

Tags are very important devices that help you add a lot of value to a big store of information. I.e. it is not that you have the information (old style non-profit) but rather how you can categorize and sort it where the value gets created.

Links

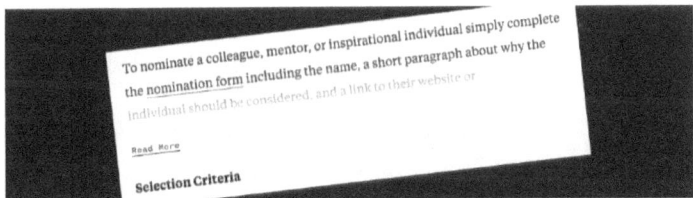

Hyperlinks or URL addresses where something can be found on your non-profit or someone else's website. These simple URL's can add a lot of value for your members by providing connections to their bios on your site, firm listings, projects and to their websites, etc. Links are what allow you to break the siloed effect of a website, which is like a magazine and extend them to become horizontally navigable based on new criteria to the ones that brought a person to the page in the first place. I.e. if someone came to view the holocaust museum, they may be intrigued to investigate who designed it or to understand more about the city it is in. These are more horizontal jumps than links that allow visitors to navigate through your website efficiently finding what interests them and therefore leading to increased page views.

Data

All digital value starts with data or information.

Data consists of facts and figures. When data is processed, interpreted, organized, structured or presented to make it meaningful or useful, the result is information. Information provides context and usefulness for data.

Numbers, text, pictures, videos, tags, member names, member firms, geographic locations, URL's. These are the basic bits of data that you must build value for members with. All sounds pretty simple but dumping a ton of data on a site is not going to do it. People don't have the time or energy to walk into a library and spend time hunting down what they need. Data is stored in databases on a modern website (think giant excel sheet with column and row position references) and folder libraries whose positions are stored in the database.

How data is categorized and optimized for search are critical to creating value. Without data, you have nothing to create value from! Think about the data you have in two ways, what does it do for members and what does it do when it is available on the Internet? Specifically, what can each piece of data do as a search term for you?

The basic difference between your website and print is that data and information are not isolated, static and frozen on the web. It is necessary to reframe your ideas about digital data as compared to the physical print world. Data and information are now stored in a database and can be controlled via code. Data can be reconfigured and presented in a thousand different ways depending on the need or question being asked. That makes it incredibly powerful as compared to print data. What you can do with that power determines how effectively you can create value for your community.

Secondly, because you can submit it all to Google (free), it enters Google's master database, is indexed and sorted according to the algorithm of their search bot and receives a page rank that places it in an order on a Google search page which then becomes an incredibly powerful way to bring traffic to your website for free and helps people find out things that they may never have known existed in your non-profit because they can now find them on the internet!

Functions - Apps/modules

A module (in Drupal an App is called a module) allows you to add new functionality to a site. Some modules operate in the background improving data handling and others on the front end add functions like a store to handle transactions, marketing, the ability to layout and change pages, add video, slideshows, draw graphs, store pictures, create your own search algorithm (i.e. so that you can make sure that your highest contributing members score better in search results on your site, etc.

In the SEGD.org example shown to produce the type of functionality that this site has requires loading over 300 Modules. Modules are incredibly powerful additions to the Core Drupal functionality. See the appendix for a full list of the modules that you will need to get to non-profit 2.0

There are thousands of modules available all for free if you are using Drupal or Wordpress. They are like Apps on an iPhone.

Configuration/Site Building

Out of the box, Drupal or Wordpress are very basic. Drupal especially is ugly and needs to be configured and customized to what you need. Once you understand the structure of Drupal it is almost infinitely customizable, which is one of its core strengths.

With Drupal, you can choose to go with a simple content driven site at first and work in stages towards complete integration of your store, AMS, Referrals system, Job bank, Events registrations, Education systems, CRM, etc.

One of the biggest things you will gain by working in this way is control over your ability to improve and customize your site, which is critical for an innovative organization. You will also gain control over your costs and the flexibility to move and change things on your website fast. In the traditional way of working for most non-profit websites, you bought a standard package from a web design firm and then had to pay to customize it, pay every time you needed any sort of changes made, so innovation did not happen because it was too expensive to continuously develop and change the site. Net result is it probably stood still for 3-5 years, hopefully no longer! That is an eternity on the web though and so your site would keep slipping back in relevance and user experience versus the professions own websites and when it came time to refresh, technology had moved on so much all you could really afford was to rebuild the site on a new technology platform, barely making any real progress on the content and functionality of the site at all.

Code

Code or software are the instructions that are used to set the rules and make the site do what you want it to do. The basic building block of a modern website is a code set called a **Content Management System (CMS** There are many open source (meaning free to use and community supported) CMS programs available today. Open source is the way to go unless you have buckets of money to throw around at a web development company for no really good reason. The choice essentially comes down to Drupal and Wordpress.

Your choice is:

- Wordpress: easier to begin using and easier to learn but more suitable to simpler sites of which non-profit site requirements are not.
- Drupal: more flexible and suitable for more complex sites such as non-profit sites but requires a time commitment to understand and learn.

The choice is yours, but after a lot of evaluation I have taken two non-profits down the Drupal route and find it highly effective for non-profits' needs. The largest trade non-profit

The National Association of Realtors nar.org, The Whitehouse whitehouse.gov, and the Economist all use Drupal, along with more than 1,000,000 other sites!

If you want to compare what technology and Content Management Systems your closest competitors are using or sites you admire, use www.builtwith.com, which will give you a full analysis of the software that they are using. It is a fantastic tool. We can attest to Drupal's much longer learning curve, but 6 years into it when we really need flexibility as we push further and further into customizing our offering, I am very, very glad we made the choice for Drupal. Many non-profits have. Drupal is free. Within 10 minutes, you can have a new website set up ready to have content added to it.

However, be aware that it will take hundreds of hours before you are where you want to be! Websites are works in progress, not off the shelf products you buy and plug in. You should be thinking about your website as a service that you have to innovate every quarter and that you will never stop innovating it as you continue to create better value for your members, but then you are probably well aware of that by now!

The great thing about code is that if you use a widely used CMS like Drupal, you have a community of thousands of coders who are constantly contributing to it, improving it and upgrading it. You can never afford that sort of progress if you go for a custom coded site where you are asking someone, can you do this or that for me?

There are three things you will want to be able to handle on your website at least. Content, users and transactions. In addition, you might need comments, data inputs and analytics. Drupal can do all of this for you. Out of the box, it is built to handle content and users. With modules which are like add-on functions you can add everything else easily enough.

An Association Management System (AMS) is a database for users' data instead of content which is handled in a CMS. Within Drupal (a Database driven CMS), you can build an AMS so that all your data content and contacts and transactions are all in a single database and all interconnected! You will want to do this so that you have full integration of your data and can take your AMS costs and start applying them directly to the continuous improvement of your website. A vital requirement to create the sort of value we are proposing in this book.

Analytics

The key difference between a print magazine and the internet is that when you post your magazine, you have no idea what happens after that. With your website, you have data available on everything that happens on the site, who is visiting, what they are doing there and what interests them. With the magazine, if you do market research, at best you will know what a small sample of readers "say" they do, not what they actually do. Your website tells you in real time if you like what your visitors do on your site when they visit.

Today there are Apps like Leadfeeder that can tell you which company the visitor is from and if they are in your marketing email system (i.e. Mailchimp or Constant Contact), it will even provide the name of the visitor to your site. These programs are great for leads and can provide a much sharper membership lead generation source for you, but they are just as useful to understand the behavior of your visitors so that you can design better paths for them to follow to reach their goals as this is a real time design research tool.

Note: This book is written for all non-profits. However, the largest non-profits can afford expensive marketing solutions and automation/customization tools such as those that are available from Adobe. The book does not discuss them or how they help as they are completely out of reach of the average non-profit.

The most important criteria - who is visiting your site? Probably over 90% are non-members. Quite possibly over 99% are not members! That can be good and bad. If you take the traditional non-profit approach that the non-profit is for the benefit of the members, you have a big problem!

But if you take a modern approach then you could say that you are generating 99% more contacts for your members than just the members visiting your site and that has a lot of value for a member as it means it is not just peers talking to each other which is the biggest misconception about an non-profit website.

What do you know about those visiting your site? Where are they going? What interests them? How do you need to further develop your content based on actual behavior (design research) rather than what people say they will do (market research)?

Digital Marketing

There are many more options to get noticed on the web, cheaper than off-line methods requiring printing, posting, follow up etc. Get into the mindset of working in a pull market, not a push market.

In a pull market, the question becomes what do I have of value that will pull people towards my website? Where do I need to make sure it is placed on the world-wide web to get attention?

Content will become a very important reason for people to visit your site, but to determine what content you need it will be necessary to go far beyond simple demographics to ask what are the wants, needs, interests, questions, concerns, and pain points of your prospects? Your content will need to be relevant, valuable and consistent for each of your customer groups. If they don't feel this attachment, they are unlikely to consider doing business or joining your non-profit.

Content Management is the new discipline that has developed and exploded around 2011. It is important because consumers have figured out how to tune out, block out and ignore advertising on the web and it has become clear that you must meet their needs for information and relevancy if you want to attract them to your website. They will not come for many other reasons, even if non-profits continue to believe (falsely) that their members find them indispensable.

Content Management involves understanding the users (of your website and non-profit) and their needs to formulate a strategy for content creation to meet those needs and a search optimization strategy to ensure that your users will find the relevant information that you have for them.

You need this discipline and its approach (pull versus push marketing) within your editorial staff to survive and thrive in the internet era. Given most non-profit editorial staff's penchant for print, you might well find that you cannot convert them and that you would be better off replacing "old ways" thinking staff with more open web savvy staff.

Failing to do this will definitely slow up the transition to an internet-based business. It is natural that staff who have been in administration mode for so long do not want to change. It is un-natural that a business is held back by staff. In the commercial world that is unthinkable. Heads would roll. You need change either in attitude or in staff. Staying the same will not deliver new ways of working, a fast innovation cycle and thinking about value creation.

Finally, a word on the value proposition of your non-profit and how that has changed in the past 5 years. Traditionally the value proposition of most professional non-profits has run something like this. We provide networking, education, information and inspiration. Today, those needs can be met (across disciplines even) by tens if not hundreds of options on the internet and in most cities with Meetup groups across the globe. They are mostly international, really international versus the average Non-profits smattering of international members.

To get 'noticed' needs a clear value proposition and most non-profit value propositions are muddier than the Mississippi in a flood. They offer only vague promises and innuendos. "You get out what we put in" and "support your professions growth", which is true for the most involved, but for the majority, the value proposition is decidedly weaker than it needs to be in a competitive environment.

There is nothing wrong with a mission to grow the profession, but then to be believable today, you need to have a clear metric to measure the annual growth, measure it every year and report back to the membership so that it is clear their support is achieving the stated mission. Just saying you do will not cut it anymore.

Brand

Brand is not visual identity. Brand encompasses what values you stand for and that determines how you behave and how they manifest themselves in a visual identity to reflect those brand values.

Brand Values

Is your brand authoritative, supportive, collaborative, nurturing? If you have not worked out what your brand stands for yet, creating a website is going to prove difficult because you have no idea what you are trying to achieve visually or in the way that the site behaves. Best sort out what your brand stands for first, it will make all the rest flow easier.

Brand Behavior

Once you know what your brand values are, you can start to translate that into brand behavior. A website is interactive and therefore it behaves a certain way when things are selected, or choices made. A great example of this is the Mailchimp site which has the brand value of being humorous and the behavior of the site reflects that humor perfectly.

Visual Identity

Your visual identity starts with your logo, but then quickly turns to the color palette of your brand, the layout: open and clean or tightly packed with information (the more open white space the better for readers usually, but that is hard to achieve on non-profit sites.

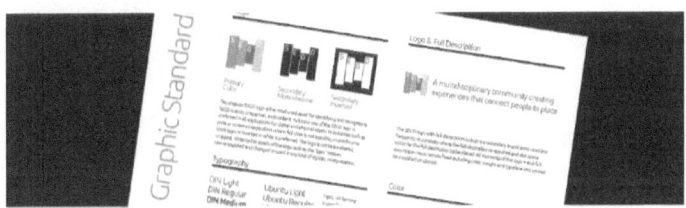

Chapter 3

How to create Digital Value for a non-profit?

Digital value is created by manipulating content, data, tools and services created using the internet. Today that means using your website and social media, but that model may well change to a much more open distribution of your content in the future.

An internet company is a commercial venture that finds a consumer insight or need, builds a digital platform to solve that need and then scales that through venture capital to try to be the first to solve that need and attract most users who have that need to their platform. Once they have a huge set of visitors the visitors are the value that attract money in the form of advertising to their platform this delivering a return on investment to the venture capitalists and hopefully a strong on-going return for the investors who buy into the IPO and pay the venture capitalists and the first-round employees back for their money and efforts. The idea is that simple and it applies directly to Non-profits just as well.

It is an important concept to grasp for non-profits.

Here are some, again, grossly oversimplified examples for the purposes of illustration of how digital value has been created:

1. Google

    a.   **Phase 1:** Identified that existing ways of categorizing the information on the web (human editors or category indexing) did not consider what readers found relevant. By thinking about what relevance meant and how to measure and weigh that they could create an algorithm to index all the content on the internet. The criteria Google analyzed proved to be a more reliable predictor of how much people value that content, i.e. the number of times keywords appeared in the body of an article, whether they were in the title, the URL, the image information and then looked at how many times people read that content, who posted links to that content, etc. The important point here was that most of the search engines that existed at that time were modeled after old world ways of categorizing content in a library, not considering the new possibilities that the internet had brought to the world. This function was offered for free to attract the largest audience to use their search platform.

b. **Phase 2:** The results appeared more relevant to people searching versus Yahoo, Microsoft and many other search engines and so people came flocking to the Google platform.

c. **Phase 3:** using the huge audience of eyeballs, they attracted most advertising on the web to their platform, thus monetizing the value of their audience. Almost all free internet businesses work per this business model: Create some form of functionality for free, gather a huge global audience and then sell access to that audience through advertising.

2. Facebook

    a. Created a forum for people to share photographs and connect friends together. The like button only came a long time afterwards where you could effectively add approvals for posts

    b. The gathered a similar global audience and because of the sheer scale of it, became highly attractive to advertisers trying to reach targeted consumers. Hence the business model that brought Facebook to profitability and a market listing was also an advertising one.

3. LinkedIn

    a. Created a platform to post your resume (a public professional identity) and let others see who you are. You can also link to other professionals and so expand the group that you can communicate with for free.

    b. LinkedIn scaled to a huge global audience of professionals and sells ads/job listings /premium access to people like recruiters who want to get to individuals as part of the hiring process. Linked in, therefore has several revenue streams. LinkedIn aims to be a global all encompassing "non-profit for everyone. With all services delivers digitally (therefore at very low cost)

There are many, many more. Instagram, Pinterest, Twitter, Asana, Uber, Lyft, etc.

For a better understanding, the internet works differently to physical channels of delivery like print, conferences and education programs. Therefore, thinking about how to create digital value will require a different approach and mindset. It requires an basic understanding at the very least of how the internet works and the tools that you have at your disposal to make value.

How can you use the components of your digital toolbox to create value for members?

1. Website traffic - Visitors
2. Users and use cases/personas
3. Search
4. Usability/experience
5. Content
6. Tagging/Filters/Taxonomies and Indexes
7. Links
8. Data
9. Functions – Apps/modules
10. Configurations/Site Building
11. Code
12. Analytics
13. Digital Marketing
14. Brand
    a. Brand Values
    b. Brand Identity

The order of the above elements may seem strange, but it is purposeful. Usually you would expect such a list to begin with data/content. It begins with Website Traffic because it is vital to think about who your data and content is for. Look at the number of visits you receive on your website today and compare that with your membership. Chances are you have many multiples of visitors more than you have members!

1. Website Traffic

This may already be one of your non-profits most valuable assets and you don't even know it!

On an e-commerce site, "traffic" is not necessarily valuable unless it is converted into sales, which in a non-profits case would mean memberships. Thinking that this is the only objective you have for your non-profit website traffic would be a big mistake. The real value of traffic visiting your website occurs when you connect it to information about your members, their firms, projects and thinking. If you are creating awareness of your members and connecting all that traffic like a signal junction yard redirecting it back out to your member's websites and providing good information about them along the way, you are creating real value for members in your role promoting the good work of your members and the profession! Your traffic is value to you as the non-profit leader, but it is not really member value until you connect it directly to the members.

How many members do you have versus how many people visit your website?

In the case of the example, SEGD only has 2,300 members. Which represents only 0.004% of the 550,000 annual unique visitors to the website! What does the proportion of members to total unique visitors look like on your website? Use Google Analytics to find this out.

If you exclude the top 10% of your member firms, based on the size of their companies. How many of the remaining 90% do you think have anywhere near the traffic that you get to your non-profit website to their own websites? You will most likely be attracting an audience much greater than 80-90% of your members, and that is even before you start to create content to attract them via search!

What is the value of your traffic to your members if you can create attention and interest in them through good profiles of the members and their work by exposing them to that huge audience? One simple answer is to use the tools provided by the Google Search Term Tool to see how much it would cost using Google Adwords to get people to your members website.

Have you ever looked at your website traffic in this way before?

Have you really thought about the fact that somewhere in the region of 95-99% of your website's traffic is from non-members?

Logically, as opposed to thinking in traditional non-profit terms, this means that you need to create value for the 99%, not for the 1% who are members! Stated differently, as we are non-profits, we have to create value for the 95-99% as well as for the membership, because there are a lot more people interested in your members and what they do than you realize.

Strategy: Ways to turn your traffic into value for your community

1. **Connect your website traffic to your members, their firms, projects and thinking.** Connect the traffic to information about your members by making this information much more prominent than the information about your non-profit i.e. move your website from the level of being an electronic brochure to becoming a content portal. This means your non-profit website would look a lot more like a corporation's website, where the information about the company is a footnote or found in the about or investor relations sections as compared to the

products or services, they sell which are front and center. You know that your non-profit is your members, not the staff, so design your digital presence to reflect that!

2. **Feed the traffic through to your member's websites.** All visitors will leave your site eventually. It is much better that they go onto your member's sites than off into the ether! From zero, in just 3 years, the SEGD.org site was able to deliver 50,000 visitors a year onto member's websites. 15% of the Non-profit's traffic! It would cost members a fortune in Google Adwords or content creation to achieve that and it is another example of how a non-profit can create value for members.

3. **Understand and quantify your visitors.** Implement a software like Leadfeeder to tell you about your visitors so that you can build profiles of who is visiting/interested in what your members.

4. **Develop tactics to convert visitors.** What are your goals as an non-profit? To grow membership? To promote the good work of members? To encourage people to participate in your events, education programs, etc.?

Tactics: How to convert your website traffic into value for your community

1. **Publish interesting content about members:** such as member bios, firms' profiles, project descriptions, videos of talks from your events, firms' news, jobs, personnel movements, etc.

2. **Search Optimize all your content!** Basic search optimization is something your staff can easily do if they know the first few simple rules about writing for

search optimization. Optimized articles will feature high in searches for member's names, firms and projects. You will find that it is highly likely that your articles provide the best information about your members in a Google search of their name! And that is exactly what you would expect from your professional non-profit in the digital age, isn't it? Having a high-quality source of information about them is good for the member but is also incredibly powerful in drawing in search to your site, thus increasing your traffic!

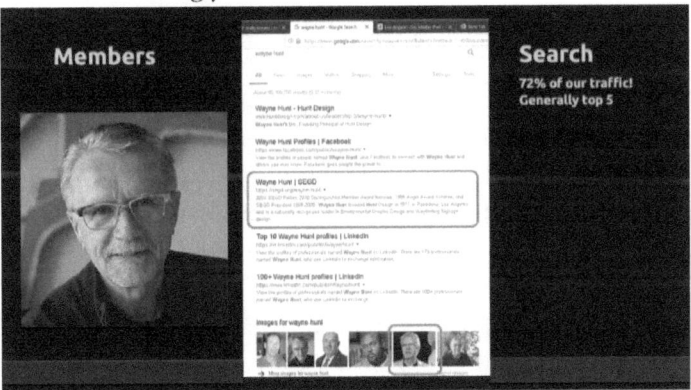

3. **Develop business intelligence** about your community

4. **Drive Outbound Links:** Push your website traffic on to visit your members' sites. They are going to leave your site at some point, wouldn't it be better that they continued to a members site than disappearing off into the ether again?

5. **Become the aggregators/curators of your professions work.** In the digital age, one of the new roles of a non-profit should be become the repository of all information about the profession. Full

descriptions or articles about all projects can act as real sources of traffic for members and their firms. If you are a member with a small firm, which will account for a large percentage of your membership, chances are they are not getting many people to their websites and therefore not a lot of broader exposure. This is borne out by the facts if you look at key search terms for your profession, you will not see many members coming out at the top of these search results even using paid Google AdWords to pull people towards their sites. You are also not that likely to see many more of your members on the top pages. Here is an opportunity for you to add value for them by making sure the Non-profit's website is highly ranked in search results (which you stand a good chance of being due to the size of the traffic to your site when you have a lot of content and scale from your membership to get you going 9 versus their own sites). As the non-profit, you need to be in the consideration set for someone searching for terms related to your profession. This is also how you draw traffic into your website, but more on that later.

6. **The power of exposure.** Your traffic is most likely vastly bigger than your membership. That means most likely the rest of the profession is taking a look at what you have got. I have found that the more they see your great new content, see how you are promoting members and their firms WHO ARE MEMBERS and notice that you are continuously improving and probably doing it much faster than most of them can do individually, they will start to see you in a very different light. SEGD's membership has climbed steady past record high numbers since the web project started in earnest. Non-profits know that

if they can get someone to participate, the chances of them staying are much higher. In some way, that is what I am are seeing with digital participation as well. Even participation and presence on your website seems to be engagement that is much better than no participation at all!

7. **Bringing the community one step closer together.** Don't underestimate the power of the bio. No one, from the CEO down really knows who all the members of a non-profit really are! So many are silent contributors or even non-contributors in the sense that they pay their dues but are otherwise disengaged and silent. When I first launched the new bios and firm listings, most of the staff did not think that it was worth the effort. Three years later and now that I have the bios integrated on the back end with the member's accounts, they complain if there is no bio so that they can see and start to get to have a visual connection to the members! Pictures and profiles are powerful, not just externally for the community! There is clear evidence of people reading an article, then going on to click on 3-5 bios of other members. Those clicks are golden for community development! When referring to Search in this book, I am always referring to organic, not paid search i.e. Google Adwords. When you see those bios rotating on the site, you are going to see members investigating who else is a member and learning what people's faces look like and what they do and starting to make virtual connections that never existed for your non-profit before in the physical networking.

Monetizing your traffic. The way of the web

This is a strategic choice. Do you monetize that amazing stream of traffic to your site or not? Depending on your traffic, it can represent a decent passive income flow if you open your site up to ads, either from Google or that you sell as part of your benefits to sponsors.

2. Users and use cases/personas

Who are the users of your non-profit and what are they trying to do by belonging to your non-profit? If you know the answers to these questions, not generically, like to network, but in detail for instance network to find a new job, or a mentor or clients, to show what you can do, etc. then you can address the building of value within the traditional idea of what an non-profit does. That would be a very good start as most non-profits go around and around talking about ideas that would address networking, learning, inspiration and information without ever solving the problem because they don't know what the problem really is.

There is, however, a new idea that needs to be considered.

Non-profits have the mandate to gain access to the most data on their profession. What problems can the most data on a profession help members or their clients solve? What other data can you collect to help them solve their problems, which leads to the fundamental question.

What problems do your users have that their non-profit and the knowledge they collect could help them solve?

Here is a (very incomplete) list, as a thought starter for brainstorming sessions of the sort of problems that the internet has solved for the world that were not possible before:

1. Make markets much more efficient.
   a. Efficiency: reducing middlemen – Amazon, etc.
   b. Connecting: bringing customers and producers together globally – Amazon, Ali-Baba, etc.
   c. Linking professionals and changing hiring – LinkedIn, etc.
   d. Creating more cost-effective education open to all – Lynda.com, etc.
   e. Creating efficient markets: Selling stuff that you no longer need. Link stuff people want to people who want it – E-Bay
   f. Efficient distribution: Turning expensive assets into revenue. The sharing economy – Uber, Lyft, Airbnb
   g. Connecting people with their friends – Facebook
2. Aggregating knowledge: Wikipedia, news sites, Flipboard, etc.
3. An always open store and sales/marketing channel: 24/7/365
4. Data and Analysis: everything is measurable and measured, all data can be gathered and processed.

The trick for finding where you can add new value is to look for any area where it feels "difficult" to do things. That is the first clue that an opportunity exists and that using the internet may help you solve a problem or create new value for your community.

Each of the above are specific use case scenarios. They each have specific users who need a specific application to solve their problem. What are the use case scenarios for your community?

3. Search

Organic search has to be the most satisfying activity! Once the ground work has been done to search optimize a piece of content and the subsequent tweaks made to get the piece to register high in searches for the term, you can sit back and watch it working for you, drawing in visitors from around the world, working while you sleep or take a week end break. It feels like you have hundreds of additional staff members working in your small marketing team! 24/7/365. Organic search is a highly efficient way to attract people interested in what your community does. People who are not aware of your non-profit but are still interested in what your members do. Just try to imagine how you would find and make these people aware of you and your non-profit before the internet. It would be impossible or at least cost prohibitive to find and serve these people.

Search Strategies:

1. As a non-profit, you have one name, one profession/industry or focus. That can be very good for focus and targeting, but not so good for arriving at viable search terms. Start by optimizing or creating content that can be optimized for the main terms that relate to your profession. To do this, you must think like a client of your members, not like a member. This means that you must think what a layman would be searching for, not optimizing for the industries terms alone. Write them all down. You should arrive at a list of about 100 terms. Categorize them into the most important ones for the profession and the ones with the largest search numbers per month and start creating content and optimizing for them. Set up a Google Adwords account and use the Google

Adwords Keyword Planner to see how many people are searching for that term a month, which is very different to how much information Google has indexed, which you see at the top of a Google search results page. You will now have to set your priorities. This will be based on which terms will bring you the most traffic, which terms are most important to win at and which terms you feel you will be able to win at! The web is big, search terms endless and therefore prioritizing is a critical step for a non-profit with limited resources.

2. Good news! You have access to a much larger pool of terms!

    a. **Members names**: Start with the leadership; your board, chapter chairs, award winners and top practitioners. Work your way through the whole membership, that will provide thousands of new search optimized terms and will drive traffic to your website in what is called the long tail effect of the web. The long tail of web activity occurs for almost all content. Initially there is a surge as it is on your home page, but then that tapers off as it slides down the gallery pages somewhere, but the trickle of traffic never really goes away and a trickle over a few years equals a flood of additional traffic when added together.

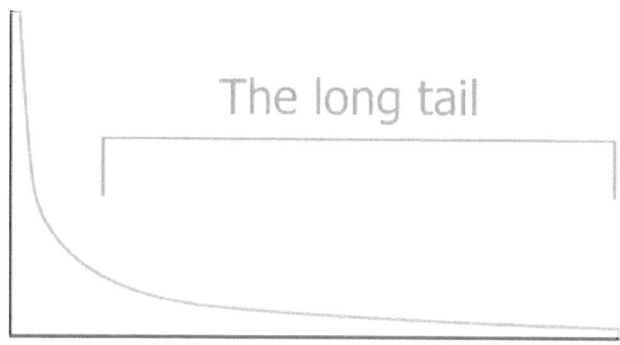

The long tail

b. **Firms names**: You probably have hundreds or thousands of firms associated with your organization, each is a potential source of traffic for you engaged in what your community does and each article about these firms is useful content to help you connect your traffic to your members firms if you have good content about them and you have search optimized that content on your website.

Example: **Airspace** designs a new entrance for **Google.** The potential keywords to optimize for in that title are bolded.

c. **Project names**: Often projects are related to places that can be optimized in the article.

Example: **3M** completes new **wayfinding** project for the **Golden Gate Park** in **San Francisco. Chapter city names**: A great search strategy is the second level of a term.

Example: people searching for wayfinding will often try to make it more specific through geography, i.e. Wayfinding **Atlanta.** Chapters are the best way to achieve this providing content for that second level search term which is usually a lot less competitive than the first.

d. **Industry terms/practice areas:** Every profession has a set of acronyms, buzz words and terms that are specific to that profession. Create content that specifically address these terms and are search optimized for them. It stands to reason that if you want to be some sort of authority, that there should be definitions of these terms available on the website.

e. **Useful links and tools from Google:**
    i.   Keyword Planner: https://adwords.google.com/home/tools/keyword-planner/ There is no need to use Adwords. You can do great work organically!
    ii. Search Term trend comparisons: https://www.google.com/trends/
    iii.

Why should you spend a lot of effort on search optimization?

In the SEGD.org example, over a 3-year period by optimizing content for search and paying attention to search as a criterion when writing content, the number of visitors from search went up 609% and the new visitors from search improved by 741%. Put in perspective the number of visitors from search went up from 35,000 to 250,000 visitors a year. Visitors from search went up from 19% of visits to 53% of visits. That would have cost at least $500,000 more to distribute magazines to all those people, and that assumes you already knew who to send them to!

Search acts as a very powerful multiplier for the effort you put into content creation.

4. Usability/experience

What value can Usability create:

1. Good usability creates positive sentiment from visitors which is the start of good relationships
2. Good site usability helps drive SEO
3. The experience of using your site determines if people want to visit again
4. Conversions

Usability strategies:

Start with software with known good Usability. Drupal for instance has spent a lot of time ensuring good usability and that counts for a lot over the 7 generations of improvements that Drupal as a platform have made versus a local web consultancy starting a new site for you from scratch!

5. Content

A lot has been written about content strategy and there are experts on the subject (like everything else in this book). From the non-profit executives' point of view the challenge and the mindset shift required is to become aware that a non-profit needs to become a content production machine in the digital age. Content is the primary tool that Non-profits can use to regain their relevance.

Whereas in the 20th century MEMBERS were the value of non-profits, in the digital age CONTENT is the value that people are attracted to first. It is a massive shift and very important to understand. With content, you can build an audience, with an audience you can either build a membership or change your business model and build advertising revenue.

Ways that content can create value:

1. Turn data into useful information for the membership
2. Well written content will be seen by people on the fringe of your membership, and be useful
3. Content is the best marketing tool to attract eyeballs to your website
4. It shines a well-crafted, appreciated light on your membership, their firms, projects and thoughts
5. It boosts your credibility and therefore your brand value
6. It can generate money for you. Content attracts visitors, visitors attract advertisers and registrations and purchases of your products and services

Content Strategies for Non-profits:

1. **From one to many:** The only way to become a content machine will be to move from having a single editor/writer producing content to most of the team producing content. Unless of course there are endless resources. (I thought not.) The membership team needs to take on the production of member bios and firm listings. The marketing team needs to produce content related to the events and education. The education team need to produce education materials, the CEO needs to be writing about the profession, thought leadership pieces and updates on the community. Get your members involved, though that will turn out to be a lot more complex than you might first imagine so be prepared that the non-profit staff will be preparing almost all the content!

2. **Agree on a style guide:** The first challenge is that there is much more content to produce than you will have professional writers to do it, so it will become necessary very quickly to have a style guide available for all to reference and work to.

3. **Creating Structure: What to write about?**

    a. In the example segd.org, one of the first exercises when working out the content strategy was to create an index of the profession because there was no structure to the content that the non-profit had on the profession. It existed in one big murky pool.

    It quickly became apparent that there were different practice areas within the community and that they addressed different industry's needs. That formed the basis of a new index created for all content that placed it within a matrix formed of practice areas and industry verticals. Once that framework was in place, it became quickly visible where the holes in the core content existed. Secondly, because everything is measurable on the internet, it was also easy to quickly see what the community was interested in which gave a view of how to think about allocating content creation resources.

    b. Members, their Firms, Projects and Thoughts. Imagine these as layers of the content cake. The structure (x/y axis) would be visible if looking down on the cake. all would be visible if you looked at a 3-D view of the cake. Awards was about the members work. The Member Bios were about the members, the Firm Listings about their firms and the Blog became clearly about thought leadership. This content really drove the search results, in many cases because SEGD is a tiny organization and they could win the top search positions for most of their members and their firms. With the long tail effect, the additional few thousand top search terms positions and the long tail effect of the web provided the huge boost in visitors.

4. **Search needs to be a big part of your content strategy**
   a. **Prioritize search terms.** Perhaps by now it has become clear that there is a never-ending stream of work to produce and obviously, a limited pool of resources with which to get it done. Therefore, prioritizing the articles and search terms that need to be optimized is a key to being effective. In a for profit venture start up, we would simply hire an army of writers and get this piece of the puzzle in place because we know it is a great investment with a huge multiplier effect to grow our visitors with. I wonder, 5 or 10 years from now when Non-profits really understand their opportunities using the internet, what percentage of revenue they might be deciding to put towards content creation?

Search Tactics: implement some simple rules

Yes, to win the big search terms requires a good deal of skill, but it is amazing how relatively easy it is to win many terms with little effort and a lot of discipline. Following a set of simple rules gets you 80% of the way to effective search. After that it takes another 80% of the effort to achieve the past 20% and it is up to you to decide if that is worth investing in. At the very least a non-profit should be doing the 20% effort internally and considering how much or in which terms they want to invest with an expert to optimize.

a. Enable English language URL's for your website, i.e. usually using the titles of your articles.
b. Ensure the Search term is in the ULR
c. Ensure the search term is in the Title
d. Ensure the search term appears 4-6 times in the content
e. Ensure that the content contains at least 200 words

6. Taxonomy: Tags/vocabularies/indexes

Taxonomy Strategies

a. **Create dynamic pages that use tags to filter content.** In this way, you provide landing pages for visitors of similar content that are all automatically generated and will create real search pull as well as being useful for your visitors.

b. **Think of tags in terms of classifications:** When you categorize tags into groups of tags called, vocabularies, such as cities, or material types, dates/times etc., the vocabularies become classifications that are searchable by visitors. They are also useful to organize content on the back end. Create a taxonomy or classification system for the profession if one does not exist so that you will be able to present the rich content on your site in many different, relevant, customized ways. For example, by industry verticals or practice areas or some specific aspect of the profession such as geography, by member firm or content by a specific member

c. **Try to determine up front what types of search/categorization would be useful to your visitors so that you can deliver a clear instruction on how to tag to content creators and keep**

usability/consistency on the site for visitors. Tag similar content/content by the same member/ firm/ geography/ material/ process etc. The uses of tagging are vast and take the thousands of pages on your site (which are like the pages in your magazine) and indexes them in a way that allows you to create alternative views of your information that are much more precise and usable for members than search. This is really where the real value of a website over a magazine or print outputs becomes very apparent. Tagging enhances the usefulness of your content and allows visitors to create their own customized pages of content that are more customized to their needs

d. **Decide whether you will enable tags to be seen and used by visitors (preferable) or not.** Tags can be presented to the user in every article, or they can be used by you as the editors to create indexes of your content that make sense to your profession

Tactics: Tags can be used in many ways to create valuable search/index structures

Filter content by geography such as a city or by topic or industry verticals or some other taxonomy or indexing system that makes sense to your members and their clients. It is a good idea to spend a lot of time thinking about the organization of your content and the taxonomy that you need to use for the profession and therefore the one that you should also use to organize (index) content on your website so that it reflects the understood concept of/organization of content for your profession. Take pains to understand how the community sees their content and try to reflect this on the website as that will then resonate best with visitors. Don't be surprised if you find there is no accepted index of information and that you land up setting it up for the profession for the first time. Consider it yet another value that you create for the profession by creating non-profit 2.0!

Filtering makes modern websites extremely powerful and allows visitors to customize their experience and the content that they find on your site to suit their needs.

I would imagine that many of you are saying to yourselves around this point. "This is all very interesting, but is this real value?" That's a question that has been asked for 20 years about the internet now and yet more and more business and value is shifting to the internet every day. It would not be doing this is it were not real value to people who visit your site. The problem with the question is not the fact that the internet generates real value, but rather that the questioner's frame of reference about what represents value is out of date!

7. Links

In the example, SEGD.org, visitors clicked links on pages that lead to member's websites over 140,000 times. That is real value being created for members as the non-profit site is acting like Google Adwords, except that the clicks a member receives are included in the price of membership!

Linking Strategies

1. **Hold traffic in the non-profit website:** A smart linking strategy would be to link member names from project or firms' content to an internal bio page for members before linking them directly to an outside link (like LinkedIn). Likewise, for firms and projects links.
2. **Create tunnels:** Use links like footnotes, except instead of providing the reference only, you can directly connect the user to the content being referenced. That means a visitor can navigate sideways across a topic (other relevant

content) and dig deep down into a topic using links. Decide how you want to use links so that there is some user consistency in linking versus using tags to connect content.

8. Data

How to think about data collection? This starts with how much resource you can allocate to data collection with the understanding that you can never collect enough data! Nor can you ever collect the right data for everyone. Whatever you have collected someone will want what you have not yet collected. Start with that assumption and it will be less painful. Also, know that when you start out the process to move to non-profit 2.0 that you probably won't place as high a priority on data as you will later when you have built the digital infrastructure to be able to cope with and use new data effectively to create value.

Data collection strategies

1. **The more data you ask for the fewer participants you will have:** deciding and asking for all the data you want to collect up front is unlikely to work. Parse it up into smaller chunks and spread the ask over time.
2. **Collect visually rich data:** It will provide you with a lot more interesting and useful content over time. Collect headshots, firm logos, project images etc. along with the basic demographic and contact data.
3. **Most everything you need about your members is on their LinkedIn profile:** But your staff are going to have to harvest because members won't.
4. **Collect what individual members can't:** naturally there is a lot of data you will need just to have the basic demographics of the profession, but allocate as much

time as you can to collecting what individual members can't like salaries, billing rates, management structures and percentages, etc.

9. Functionality – Modules/apps

The type of functionality needed depends on the level of your website. On-line brochure? Collection of non-profit management tools? Content publisher? Digitally enabled non-profit with a full suite of membership tool - Non-profit 2.0

Features of a website for a non-profit 2.0

1. Top Level Features

a. All non-profit management functions run on a single Content Management System (CMS) (Drupal recommended) which also drives the website, CRM, AMS, Store.

b. Responsive site, mobile enabled

c. SEO optimized architecture

d. Dynamic page construction. Dynamically generated pages bring a whole new level of flexibility to the use and building of your website. They are essentially landing pages for tagged content. I.e. Firms and member bios. On these pages, all content from the websites various content pools are filtered and presented as those in which the member is tagged in our case that means their contact details (visible to members only), News, their bio and headshot, awards they have won, research they have done, Feature articles they have been referenced in, blog articles on/by them.

e. Random rotations of Member Bios/Firm Listings/Awards (projects) on every page of the website. on every page of your site rotating randomly.

Once people have read the article they came for, these rotations connect them to your community. (before they go on to more relevant content, get them to investigate one member of the community or one firm! That is more valuable to the community.)

    f.   T-shaped Content Structure. Wide, shallow first level gallery or landing pages with deep, rich, focused second level gallery or landing pages

    g.   Integrated Blog, Forums, Galleries, Awards Management Module, CMS, AMS (Association Management System), Jobs, Member Directory and Store.

        i.   Benefits: single sign in for everything

       ii.   Single update of information shared and sharable everywhere with permission assignment to different groups such as board/members/visitors.

    h.   Advanced site search with the ability to add criteria like member's value spent with the organization/sponsors/years of membership/volunteer leadership contributions/etc. to the search weighting (algorithm) for more relevant (to the organization/membership) search results.

    i.   Advanced permissions control for Admins/Chapter Chairs/Board/Members/Purchasers

    j.   Chapter CMS. The ability for each chapter to post content; blogs/notices of events, news about their local members etc.

2. Content/Articles:

    a.   Feature articles (in depth about projects/Firms' members)

    b.   Member News articles

    c.   Members Bios (profiles) articles

    d.   Firm Listings (profiles) articles

    e.   Awards articles

    f.   Events articles

    g.   On-line/webinar recordings Courses

    h.   Research articles

    i.   Education articles

    j.   Integrated Video windows

3. Contacts

    a.   Individual contacts

        i.   Members

        ii.   Lapsed

        iii.   Contacts

    b.   Firms contacts

4. Landing Pages

    a.   Awards Gallery

    b.   Events

    c.   People

    d.   Firms

    e.   Projects Galleries

    f.   Chapters

    g.   Explore Galleries

    h.   Education

    i.   About

    j.   Store

    k.   Courses

    l.   Research

    m.   Members individual Blog pages

5. Taxonomy: Tags/vocabularies/indexes

    a.   Tags. i.e. New York

    b.   Vocabularies, collections of tags. i.e. US city names

    c.   Indexes. i.e. geographic index.

6. Integrated store

    a.   Product catalog

    b.   Discounts

    c.   Licenses

7. Marketing Support
    a.   Google Analytics

    b.   Google Webmaster tools

    c.   Leadfeeder, visitor analytics

A feature list is dry and lifeless. Ask any marketer and they will tell you that you need to sell the sizzle, not the steak. I.e. the Benefits of the feature, not the feature itself.

10. Configurations/Site Building

Strategy: keep it flexible by configuring from the front-end Drupal tools of blocks/views/articles and nodes.

With an open source technology like Drupal, you have the front-end tools at your disposal to build pages, blocks or areas on a page and content types to suit your needs that are flexible and modifiable thereafter. If you use a web development firm, the first thing they will want to do is hard code your framework or structure. It is more efficient to build the site by hard coding in PHP (popular general purpose scripting language that powers everything from your blog to the most popular website in the world) but it means that unless you have PHP coding skills in your team that you will require a web development group to help you make any changes. At least for the first few years, it is much better to build the site from the front end of Drupal so that for the most part (There will be things you can't do this way) you can maintain control of the site building and therefore your ability to prototype and change cheaply and quickly internally. Resist the "this needs to be coded" strongly and if you are not building it yourself, force them to build the configuration with the Drupal front end tools of panels, blocks and views.

Web consultants have a big vested interest in trapping you into a lot of maintenance and upgrade work which all needs coding. It is also more interesting and challenging for them, but it is not their site and your duty is to your members: build more efficient tools and a platform that can easily be innovated and modified. The non-profit website must evolve and improve for them without the need to keep hiring in web developer services to do basic site configuration work.

Reserve your budget instead to do the complex work (which the web developer will appreciate as it is interesting challenging work for them) and you will appreciate because instead of doing the simple, they will be contributing to real advances in the way that your site works. This way you can train many of your staff to be able to work with these elements and therefore bring the control and more mundane modifications of your site into the staff function at a much lower development cost than the typical $150 an hour that a web development firm will charge.

Bringing site configuration work into the staff function is the way to get all staff learning the basics of website building and structures and helping them to get comfortable with prototyping/experimenting and building new functionality. In addition, it is a huge cost saving and shifting from "we need a consultant to do this" to "we can do it" is one of the necessary changes in thinking required to become an non-profit 2.0. Building a complex site will run into the hundreds of thousands of dollars now days. Doing a lot of the web building/configuring work in house can hold costs down to the tens of thousands to build the site and the same to keep it upgraded every year.

11. Code

Strategy: Aim for the least possible!

The more you customize your site from the original download, the more code will need to be written specifically for you. This is where it starts to get expensive, so think carefully whether you need to customize things. Ask if it is necessary or simply that it is a different "new" way of working. If an non-profit is used to working a certain way, they will struggle to change and to see that there are other ways to achieve the same thing! Therefore, it is up to the non-profit executive to understand the difference between "doing things the way we always have and actual differences in functionality. The goal should be to customize as little as possible, knowing a certain amount is always going to be necessary, but treat it like administering drugs. You want to administer as little as humanly possible!

What customer value can you create with code?

Anything you want. Every website is built on code that creates certain functionality, so the simple answer is whatever you can imaging, the more complex one is you can solve real problems or needs that you community have from connecting, to knowledge sharing to inspiration. It will cost you, but this is where you become a completely different non-profit 2.0 organization.

12. Analytics

Internal Strategy 1: Understand your visitors

The difference between market research and design research is that market research asks people what they would do (i.e. helps understand preferences) and design research observes what they do (observes actual behavior). Design research delivers better insights from which to design new solutions to meet people's needs and problems. Analytics tell you what people are doing or how they are behaving; therefore, it is informative to view analytics not as numbers, but more like real time design research of the entire user base! From your analytics, you can develop well informed (rather than theoretical) use cases.

Internal Strategy 2: Understand the machine - measure your progress

Everything is measurable on the web. Therefore, it is necessary to decide what needs to be measured and for what reason. Remember the web (at least for Non-profits who are not venture funded to buy advertising to pull people towards their websites) works on the pull marketing model. Therefore, the goal is to ensure that you have put content in the places where people who are interested in what you do will find it and that means primarily search optimization. Measuring the teams Search Optimization efforts will be one of the primary analytic measurements.

Track the general metrics of your site so that you are aware of what articles are piquing people's interest, where you are growing, which sections are popular and where your traffic is coming from. Probably not as much from the social media as everyone is telling you! Set up paths with Google Analytics so that you can measure the effectiveness of your marketing campaigns and understand the conversion rates from promotion to registrations, memberships and other sales. All this information helps you to move away from the unmeasured, laissez–faire method of Non-profits to a more scientific data-based type of marketing more akin to the ways that modern businesses operate.

Analytics are very important to measure the effectiveness of your inputs, the ROI and the progress you are making. In

Chapter 8 there are a lot more details on the tools you can use and what metrics they can provide you with.

What customer value can you create with analytics?

External Strategy 1: create understanding. Analytics can help your members to build an accurate picture of the profession though understanding what is trending, what is interesting the profession and what resources they are looking for. You can do this using the analytics from your site as well as researching google analytics for the web in general to help build a picture of what people are searching for in respect to your profession.

External strategy 2: Rankings. Top 5/10/20. Rankings are a way that you can use to draw attention to firms, projects and members. It is amazing how people are drawn to top lists!

13. Digital Marketing

The purpose of this book is to explain how to see the internet differently, more as a problem solving, value creation tool for non-profits. There is plenty of information available on how to use websites, social media, blogs and forums for marketing a non-profit.

The only point to make here is that you are now in control of modifying your site, so you can design paths, insert call to action blocks and design links to feed people through the marketing stages of awareness, interest, desire and action throughout your site. Use your analytics to understand where people are coming in and design the interventions on those pages needed to feed people to desired results. If the desired results don't happen, then use your analytics to discover why. In this way, your website becomes your laboratory and prototyping shop. Play, and learn, learn, learn!

Over the last decade web technology, especially CMS software has made incredible progress, become widely and freely available.

Web 3.0 involves smarter marketing. It is about customizing the experience and content for individuals visiting your site and maximizing the conversion to action. As of writing most of the tools that deliver the data you need for customizations are not available in an affordable form for most non-profits. They are there (Adobe SiteCore, etc.) But with very high license fees and site build fees running a million plus, they will only be available to the largest non-profits.

Expect this to change in the next 5 years though as the signs are already there. For instance, Aquia, a large Drupal development consultancy has already built a similar marketing tool for Drupal, but it is definitely not free.

Keep an eye open and track the progress of developments in customization for Open Source software systems very closely. Enter as soon as you can and get on the learning curve!

14. Brand

For many new to your organization, the website is likely to be their first point of contact, so how the site responds to their needs, how easy it is to navigate, what it looks like and how it makes them feel (supported, or lectured to?) will determine how they think about the non-profit. Getting your website right is that important!

As with marketing, it is not the intention of this book to go into brand strategies and tactics except to say that it may be time to force a change in culture. Look around your non-profit and evaluate how much is spent on postage, printing, design and publication of physical materials and ask why?

There is no paper version of Wikipedia/Facebook, LinkedIn, Google, Uber, Airbnb store? Amazon (well a few stores only!). Kayak, Expedia, Whitehouse.gov? Stopping what you are doing physically and transferring it to digital is where you will be able to get a lot of the resources needed to become an internet 2.0 organization. This may be the hardest for you to absorb and decide to do, but like it was critical in the 'Race for Relevance' to change your governance, I believe it is as important to make a clean break with physical marketing to change the mindset and attitudes in your non-profit. If AIGA, the non-profit of graphic design (mainly print design) can stop their magazine and go to digital publishing – so can you!

Someone much smarter than me once told me that all marketing innovation on the internet starts on the porn sites. That is just wrong! As the most under-capitalized organizations, it should be that all new marketing innovations come from non-profits! It's time to get working on fixing this.

Chapter 4

Developing a value creation competence

How do for profit companies continuously create new value?

In the 20th century non-profits had few and in most cases no competitors.

In the Internet enabled 21st century, you probably have hundreds if you count all the bloggers out there. Mostly they will not be as big as you are or offer as many services, but they are acting very differently (hint: they are for profit companies) addressing sharply defined niches and constantly chipping away at your relevance.

Remember back in the last century how we used to talk about Tech companies as something different and special, how we knew that they ran faster, innovated faster than other firms, had massive innovation capacities and were expected to do more for less EVERY YEAR? They were efficiency monsters chewing up competitors in the non-Internet world who did not keep up. In a world where the main market is a single global access point, the internet, it is vital to build your platform fast and attract the audience to your website before they find someone else's site and don't come back to you.

Have you have ever stopped to consider that today practically EVERY firm is a tech firm because tech has affected us all and therefore if you are not thinking and acting like a tech firm and have not built staff competences like a tech firm that you are most likely going backwards relative to your more tech savvy competitors!

Sadly, non-profits have been in a type of reality distorting bubble for the past 20 years, not innovating or moving with the times as far as the use of digital technology is concerned and for that reason, they often find themselves wondering about their relevance today. Not surprising given the 20 years of innovation that has occurred in for profit firms around your non-profit. And here I am thinking specifically about your own member's firms!

This chapter outlines how the playing field has changed and what you will need to do in order to respond and rekindle your non-profit's relevance to your members. This book assumes that you have already read The Road to Relevance by Harrison Coevner and Mary Byers which gives a very good account of how you will need to change your governance in order to become nimbler and more reactive.

The central theme of this chapter is that non-profits, in their present form, are essentially administrative organisms not set up to understand customers and create new products and services. They are not designed to identify, understand and meet the ever changing and rapidly diversifying needs of their markets, nor are they capable of understanding, manipulating and implementing new digital technologies to address those needs. By addressing this value creation capability gap in your non-profits thinking, strategies structure and competences, you will be able to reposition your organization to better cope with the rate of value creation going on around you that is whittling away at your relevance and over time rebuild your relevance.

If you are familiar with the processes and methods that most for profit companies use to create products and services, such as left/right brain thinking, user centered Design Thinking, Product Management and understand Marketing as much, much broader than just marketing communications, then skip this chapter. However, I suspect that for many who have mainly worked in the non-profit world, this chapter may be the most crucial for you to gain an understanding of the types of skills and competences that you will need to add to your staff or develop from within existing staff (highly unlikely) in order to become a different, modern value creation machine capable of becoming more relevant to your members.

Most non-profit executives will immediately think, oh, I can just buy this in as consulting services, but I will argue strongly, based on a world of proof that the strategy of buying in the core competence and function of your very survival has never produced any for-profit company of any significance and it will not do so in the not for profit non-profits either.

The time has come to rethink what a non-profit is and rebuild yours with a new skill set that will help future proof its ability to create value for members.

Why is it important to develop creation competences?

Value Creation in the 21st Century

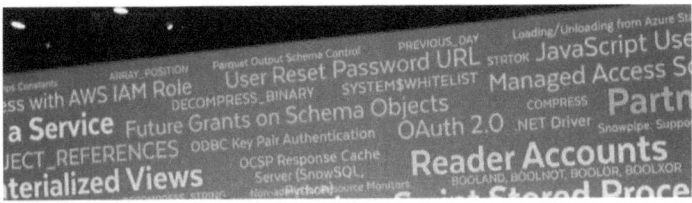

Characteristic 1: Constant, relentless change. Think of introducing new benefits or upgrading features every quarter.

Characteristic 2: Freely or cheaply available digital technologies accessible to all,

Characteristic 3: Digital technologies are relatively cheap and easy to manipulate with minimal resources.

Characteristic 4: Customization and user experience are paramount to generating useful benefits for members.

Characteristic 5: Digital platforms have real time feedback loops that provide the ability to constantly learn about your members needs and preferences.

You probably aren't hearing this from your present technology providers, but then hopefully you have noticed they are operating in an old fashioned closed (niche market) way servicing non-profits only?

Most for profit corporations are now constantly evolving, rapidly in many cases. Gone are the days of making an innovation in a product or service that you can live off for a decade. How long have you been offering your annual conference, magazine, education program, awards, chapters, journal, member directory or even your present website? I thought so!

Due to the constant changes in technology and rapid globalization of markets which change a corporation's ability and the speed at which they can create new user value, do you still believe that you will be able to afford to buy in the competences and services that you will need to evolve constantly? And even if you could, who's building the knowledge and experience in that way of working? In the age of the Internet, non-profits must be able to create new value themselves constantly to become competitive and more relevant to their community.

What is missing from a non-profit's competence/skill set versus great for-profit corporations?

The Creation Function.

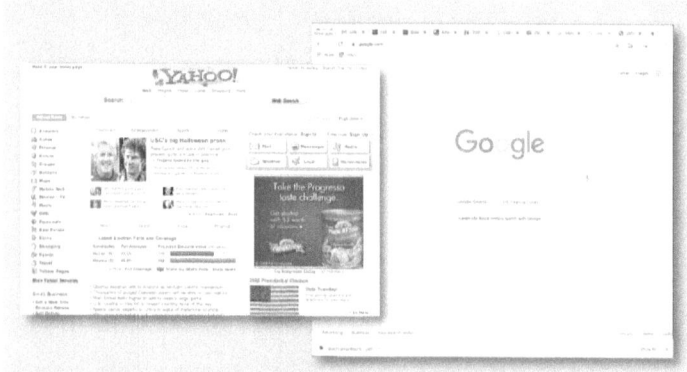

The most important function missing from non-profits today is the creation function which in for-profit corporations consists of at least 3-4 competences: Design, Product Management, Development and Marketing. Of the four, arguably, design is the most important for its ability to drive innovation through a different way of thinking about value creation.

In Silicon Valley and across all traditional management consultancies, design has become a core competence in supporting client's innovation improvements. Design and technology go hand in hand. No company succeeds today without both working well together.

Design Competence

Non-profits for the most part only meet the lowest level use of design, that of making stuff look better, but that is not real design at all. In recent DMI (Design Management Institute research), it is calculated that companies that only use design tactically miss about 70% of the value created by design used strategically (as a core competence of and top-level activity in an organization.

Few get to really experience the power of design because they are not prepared to or more likely do not understand how to engage design at a strategic level and experience it working the way that great design does to clearly build all functions and services of the non-profit around the users rather than around the non-profit and its staff. Design used in this way at the problem-solving level has been shown to increase the value of

Fortune 500 Companies by about 220%. I am sure your community would appreciate that!

What is the difference between art and design and between design and design thinking?

Art is the use of creativity for personal expression or to reflect or comment on how the artist perceives the world and the culture around them.

Design is the use of a person's creativity to solve problems for other people, usually customers.

Design is problem solving, Art is personal expression.

Design involves two aspects, thinking or a problem-solving methodology and craft – making or doing.

Great designers have a very refined high level of craft which can make them appear to be amazing artists, but that is only 30% of what they are! All non-profits employ design today for its craft. Since the industrial revolution (when craftsmen were replaced by machinery) design has been viewed as a sort of craft in the employ of industry to make products and services look better than the engineers and coders of the software that drive the machines of mass production can achieve.

Over the past half century Design has evolved rapidly to be able to articulate the differences (abductive or lateral, versus deductive or linear logical thinking) between it and other business processes, to the point where today even the US government has a special department, The Lab@OPM, within the Office of Personnel Management (OPM) to develop Design Thinking skills and roll that program of learning out to all government departments as a core competence.

Design Thinking as a process is characterized by:

1. A user centered focus. Design puts the user at the center of the process always asking what does the user need? Not what do we need, what profit do we need to make, how will we produce this. Those all must be solved, but ONLY after you are clear on what user requirements you are trying to meet.
2. Rapid prototyping and iteration of ideas. Fail fast, learn fast and early while it does not cost much. The goal is to test, learn and modify ideas early before committing to expensive development activities.
3. Test with users early so you have real world information to base decisions on.
4. Abductive thinking as well as logical thinking. The Design Thinking process encouraged wild leaps of imagination to influence the process, not just logical thinking which dramatically increases the chances of break-through, innovative ideas emerging.

Design Thinking as a process to solve problems is most clearly illustrated by the D School's Design Thinking Process. (http://dschool.stanford.edu/redesigningtheater/the-design-thinking-process/)

We are all DESIGNERS!

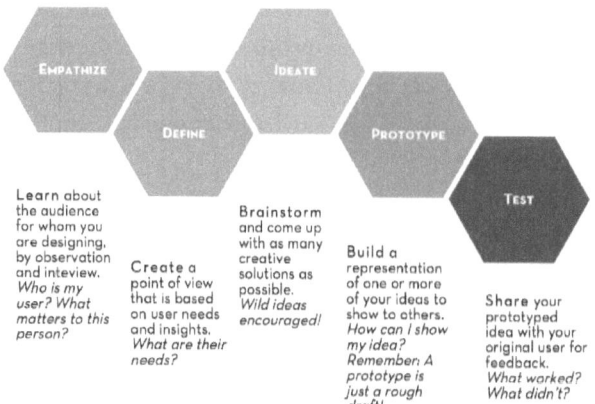

EMPATHIZE

DEFINE

IDEATE

PROTOTYPE

TEST

Learn about the audience for whom you are designing, by observation and inteview. *Who is my user? What matters to this person?*

Create a point of view that is based on user needs and insights. *What are their needs?*

Brainstorm and come up with as many creative solutions as possible. *Wild ideas encouraged!*

Build a representation of one or more of your ideas to show to others. *How can I show my idea? Remember: A prototype is just a rough draft!*

Share your prototyped idea with your original user for feedback. *What worked? What didn't?*

There are 5 steps in the D School design thinking process

EMPATHIZE: Work to fully understand the experience of the user for whom you are designing. Do this through observation, interaction, and immersing yourself in their experiences.

DEFINE: Process and synthesize the findings from your empathy work in order to form a user point of view that you will address with your design.

IDEATE: Explore a wide variety of possible solutions through generating a large quantity of diverse possible solutions, allowing you to step beyond the obvious and explore a range of ideas.

PROTOTYPE: Transform your ideas into a physical form so that you can experience and interact with them and, in the process, learn and develop more empathy.

TEST: Try out high-resolution products and use observations and feedback to refine prototypes, learn more about the user, and refine your original point of view.

The Design Thinking process oscillates between convergent and divergent thinking as you go through the process.

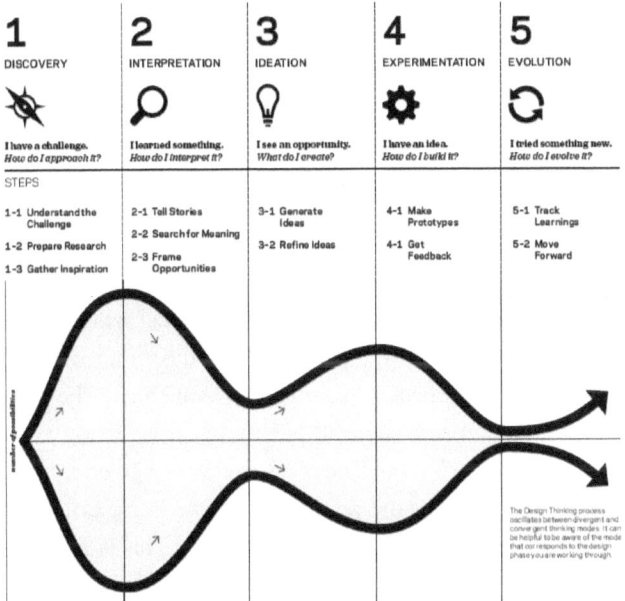

1	2	3	4	5
DISCOVERY	INTERPRETATION	IDEATION	EXPERIMENTATION	EVOLUTION
I have a challenge. How do I approach it?	I learned something. How do I interpret it?	I see an opportunity. What do I create?	I have an idea. How do I build it?	I tried something new. How do I evolve it?

STEPS

1-1 Understand the Challenge	2-1 Tell Stories	3-1 Generate Ideas	4-1 Make Prototypes	5-1 Track Learnings
1-2 Prepare Research	2-2 Search for Meaning	3-2 Refine Ideas	4-1 Get Feedback	5-2 Move Forward
1-3 Gather Inspiration	2-3 Frame Opportunities			

The Design Thinking process oscillates between divergent and convergent thinking modes. It can be helpful to be aware of the mode that corresponds to the design phase you are working through.

No company that wants to be great today can hope to compete without a design function. Design is core to all successful digital technology companies and has to become so for all non-profits as well.

For starters, you need designers on staff, and you will need to learn a whole new way of problem solving! However, the best news is that it is also going to be fun and bring a whole new level of inspiration to your staff who will feel empowered and energized at the prospect of advancing.

Product Management Competence

For profit companies that produce a product or service have a function called Product/Service Management.

The purpose of this function is to understand the corporation's potential users' needs and the corporation's capabilities (specifically its technological capabilities) and in partnership with their design/creative function to arrive at new solutions to meet users' needs in a measured continuous manner plotted on a roadmap of expected improvements over a series of years!

A large part of this role is the development of roadmaps that lay out when the technologies will be available and how to cluster them into products or feature bundles that will solve targeted customers' needs at a price that the customer will be willing to pay for the product/service and available at the place where they want to buy it. It is easy to write this down but given the number of variables that must be juggled into a workable compromise or the amount of effort to maximize each criterion, it is incredibly hard to get right. This is the function at which Steve Jobs really excelled, mainly because he used his personality and incredible vision to drive this process forward!

The second role that they perform is to deal with how to bring these solutions to market effectively and efficiently. Product Management is the planning, distribution strategy function to design and developments imagination and creation functions.

Working together with Design, their output is the price, the product or service and the place part of marketing. All that remains is the promotion, for which you already have staff to support that function.

Development Competence

The Development function in a corporation is responsible for taking the plans of Product Management and the designs for services from Design and realizing them in a reliable, dependable way so. They reduce the risk of failure of service from the product or service and thus disappointment or worse from the users. Development is also responsible for understanding and introducing new technologies to the organization. Development comprises the skills of engineering and quality control.

These three disciplines (along with R&D in the case of advanced technology companies) are the core value creation functions of a corporation. Non-profits need to include the service creation competences in their staff function if they are to survive and thrive in the new era of competition.

Do you have a function like this in your non-profit or are you depending on your program (read project) management staff? If not, which is most likely in most non-profits, hopefully it might now start to become apart why it has been so hard to successfully redesign the non-profit this century and to remain or even improve your relevance.

The answer, most likely is that this is something you outsource. However, no major brand or corporation exists that outsources its core value creation function. Many support the Value Creation Services through consultancy services, but all invest heavily in ensuring that their creation functions are world class.

Without great product management, design and development skills, no amount of great marketing is going to make you successful. Truly great products, those which meet real users' needs in a compelling easily useable and appealing manner pretty much sell themselves. Most mediocre products need a lot of marketing push to drive them through the channels to a sale. Recognize that way of marketing?

Which way would you rather exist? With great products that your users want or forever having to pedal mediocrity on your audience? Ask your Membership Director which model they are working with at present?

Sadly, the reality of most non-profits today, who are in commercial terms; under financed, under-staffed and grossly under skilled in the creation area, is that they are confined to the role of pedaling mediocrity. But it does not have to be that way if you reallocate some resources and start to build into your thinking that you have to have creative resources to survive long term and as your mandate is to be in this for the long term, that would seem like a fairly easy strategic decision to make.

Surprisingly, non-profits tend to think of themselves as different to corporations, but they are not and especially in the age of the internet are increasingly coming into competition with corporations. Both exist to create some sort of value that a user would want. If they do not, they die. It is their sole reason for existing.

The only difference between them should be that a corporation pays its investors back for their contributions to finance the corporation and a not for profit organization pays its members, who are also its users. Oversimplified, perhaps, but necessary to help you see there should be very little difference between the functions within each of these value creation machines.

The differences are in how they are financed, not what they are or the kind of organizational structures and competences they have. And yet, today non-profits are far, far from efficient, competent value creation machines. For the most part, they look much more like administrative organisms or government departments, taking care of legacy programs started 30-100 years ago!

It is up to us, the leaders of non-profits to address this issue. We can do that very easily by rethinking our priorities and where we invest the scare resources of the non-profit.

We need to change the skills and competences that non-profits have on staff so that we have the ability, as do corporations, to develop new value constantly to help us become more relevant for our members.

Marketing Competence

The goal of marketing is to "sell Jane Smith what Jane Smith wants, where she wants it, when she wants it and at the price she wants it."

So often though, it is not possible to answer all of these requirements truthfully or with any real knowledge of the non-profit's community. THAT is why it is difficult to sell the programs and therefore non-profits landing up investing heavily in marketing communications to overcome the challenges of promoting the areas where there are no clear answers! It would be much more effective to apply the same investments to understanding the consumer and their needs as that is an investment in long term marketing knowledge about the consumer that will pay back handsomely over time as opposed to continuously having to reinvest in pushing products that are not quite what the community needs.

In comparison, and it is a grossly unfair comparison for many reasons, but useful to illustrate the difference nonetheless, how much did Facebook, Google or LinkedIn have to promote to you before you used them? AND I did not even know before I did use them that I even needed them!

The 4 P's of Price, Product, Promotion and Place is definitely feeling dated as the structure of marketing, but never the less still a very useful framework to understand the marketing function and a very good guide as to the type of competences you will need to go from a marketing as communications role to a full marketing competence.

The trio of Design, Product Management and Development take care of the product, the price and often the place where those leads will come from. In a non-profit it would be useful to think of the role of place (distribution) and promotion as a single "marketing" role.

Many non-profits have a role referred to as Communications, but it gives a false expectation in many cases of what is needed. The role of Communication means corporate communication or public relations and I think that is how most communication managers/directors view their role in Non-profits as well. The problem is that what a non-profit needs is promotion more than corporate communications and it sets up the function of promotion incorrectly as a soft sell rather than a targeted hard sell role. For non-profit 2.0 to work, it would be much better to define this role as a marketing role responsible for promotion as well as public relations.

Apply the Jane Smith concept to your non-profit and you will very quickly identify in which area you have a marketing problem. In all likelihood, right now, it might be all of the above requirements or at least many of them, making the work of marketing that much more complex.

To start with, it states that to succeed, you are ONLY selling something to Jane Smith, not every possible segment of a market as we have to in non-profits who's role is defined in gravity defying, or at least business common sense defying terms as we have to please everyone all the time.

Of all the complex issues that have to happen to become a non-profit 2.0, defining exactly whom you are going to serve is most likely going to be the most difficult. Especially seeing as you probably need your board to agree that you do not have to cater to every segment of your profession. However, determining this will give your staff a newfound focus and a real direction to work towards.

Chapter 5

Becoming User Centric

Applying the methodologies of Design Thinking to Non-profits

Design is the only profession in the product creation process that puts the user right at the center of their activity and then creates a process to understand the user, to emphasize with them and to create solutions that work for them.

What is Design?

Design is the process of applying creativity to solve other people's problems. It is partially an act of self-expression, but mainly a problem-solving endeavor. In a modern context the role of a designer is to harness technology for the use of people. Many of the things that designers do involve creating an appealing engaging interface between a user and technology, whether that is a chair, potato peeler, book, or website. Designers are part of a team of people who specify, invent and innovate technology. Practically no designer can work alone. As technology gets more and more complex, so to do the teams of people who collaborate to make these products possible. Websites are at that level now days. A single designer is OK for the most basic of brochure ware sites, but as you move past that to create some form of functionality on the site, you very quickly need coders, information architects and many more.

What trips most people up design is confusing "design" with the artifact. The product is not the design. It is one of the outputs of the design process, the craft part of the process that requires high degrees of skill, practice and refinement to deliver world class results. The other part is what is now called Design Thinking.

What is Design thinking?

Design thinking refers to certain design centric activities applied in the process of designing. The process of design. About 20 years ago it became clear that the design process was mature, repeatable and offered more reliable results than "innovation" which has a 90% failure rate as opposed to the design process that has a success rate of probably over 90%.

Design Thinking, much like the planning process of Product Management aims to bring together what is desirable for users with what is technologically feasible from the producer.

The Design Thinking process consists of Research/Emphasize, Define, Ideate, Prototype and Test.

Some of the notable differences between Design Thinking and Engineering/deductive/logical thinking are the upfront research to understand users and their needs and to empathize with them in the context of using the solution, the fast fail early and quick prototyping to understand how a solution is working, especially this methodology applied to users to see their reactions, not just those of the team building the product and the quick incremental improvement cycles of design before any commitment is made to tool the product or code a website where the real costs start.

If you employ a real designer capable of problem solving and unlocking insights about how users will use your data and website, you will be in the very best position to make the best use of your organizations very scarce resources.

105

What does it mean to be user centric? Aren't Non-profits already user centric?

Clearly non-profit professionals understand that members own the non-profit and treat them somewhat differently than a customer of an organization, but for the most part, non-profits are definitely not user centric yet. Most have few feedback loops to effectively use customers' inputs to redesign and innovate their programs and most likely no upfront processes to trial out solutions with users in their context before committing them to programs. Most of which have been pretty much the same format for decades despite rapidly changing circumstances.

Do you really have a good grip on the problems your members face on a daily basis?

How does a user centric approach change the way you think as a non-profit?

Most non-profits have education programs that are attended by 5-10% of Non-profits members if they are well run. Many are attended by fewer. In order to get those attending to the programming probably requires quite a bit of marketing push on your part. In a user centric non-profit where the programs have been designed around real user needs, the users would be participating in much larger numbers and probably would not require half as much marketing effort to get there seeing as you are answering a real need for them. We have a long way to go in becoming more user centric. It is a journey, not a destination. By the way, it is worth asking yourself why you are applying scarce non-profit resources to programming that will only be taken advantage of by less than 5% of the membership when you have a website that is probably appealing to something like a thousand times the size of your membership. Where should you apply your scarce resources for the maximum benefit to the community?

Understanding why the website is appealing to so many more people would be the first step on the road to becoming more user centric. Making changes on the site to see how that effects traffic would be the second step! Rapidly trying different things would mean you are on the road to implementing a User Centric Design Thinking process to value creation! Next, you'll be challenging Apple or Facebook for dominance!

The Central Question is:

How might we understand the needs of our members, design a system that scales cheaply and cost effectively, uses digital technologies and meets more of our members needs making us more vital and relevant to their success and the success of their corporations and firms?

Chapter 6

Case Study: First steps creating digital value

20 Ideas to leapfrog your non-profit into non-profit 2.0

The case study example SEGD, the Society for Experiential Graphic Design, is a small 2,300-member $1,850,000 annual revenue non-profit with a staff of 9. 90% of the work to build this website was done in house with 10% support from some expert Drupal Developers able to solve some of the more complex coding/configuration problems to support the staff.

The initial site was built for an external support cost under $10,000 while the non-profit was struggling to return to the black after the 2008 recession. For the past 3 years, a budget of $35,000 (still only 2% of budget) was been allocated for external technical development from year 2 and started to innovate more heavily after the initial build. On the old site one staff member was acting as a webmaster, adding content only. No significant development of the site had taken place for the 5 years that it had been in existence.

With the development of the new site through 2013 and launch in Jan 2014, all staff members were helped to understand how to use the CMS through internal training and now contribute content, development ideas and support to the site. Innovations are released every few weeks.

The AMS, previously a Filemaker database has been integrated directly into the Drupal website so that all data (contacts, articles, videos, images) are run through the same database allowing for unbelievable flexibility and opportunity to combine data in ways that can generate new value for members. For example, by using the total amount that a member has contributed (in $ terms) as one of the search criteria on the website thus bringing a Google relevance level of sophistication to the sites search that rewards members of long standing who have been loyal to the organization.

One of the most powerful changes that have occurred in the staff through the course of this project is that having taken back control of the technology that the website is developed on and having spent time to understand it, the staff have started to feel empowered to ask what problems the members have and imagine how the data and digital assets that now have been developed can help them solve their problems. This is leading to a very different proactive way of thinking about how to develop the non-profit. In fact, what it is now really becoming:

User Centric

What problem do your non-profits' users have?

It's important that you edge your staff's mindset much closer to that of a web start-up with a strong user centric approach to value creation.

Much more time is being spent understanding user problems and armed with the Design thinking process to guide the development, it assists in asking questions like:

How might our data delivered through our website solve our users' problems?

So much was found out about our members that led s to the first design of the website. Started the process using design thinking and asking the question: who are we targeting and what problems do they have that we can create a service or feature to help them solve their problems with, thus making our non-profit more valuable and relevant for them?

This case study is presented as a series of insight that was gained during the process that I am sure will have wide relevance to all Non-profits and ideas that were implemented. Some will work for your members' others may not be quite the right idea. Use the insights to give you a head start and ask if the idea is the right solution for your membership or not. If they are implemented right away and start creating value, is not quite right spend some time to see how to rethink them to work for your members.

Insight one.

This came in an ah-ha moment when I looked at the website visitor's statistics. I realized that many multiples more visitors coming to the non-profit website than most of our members have going to their own websites through the established brand name effect of familiarity and name recognition with the non-profit, plus a lot of good content.

It helped me realized that this traffic is an asset that you can use to help your members.

What I found out was that in the research phase that only 0.4% of the annual unique visitors were from the actual members - if every member visited the website!

This insight really started me thinking down a very different path to the design of the last website, which was a very elegant on-line brochure with a store attached. In Design Thinking fashion, we must ask ourselves:

How might this traffic asset be applied to help members?

As alternatives to social media and Adwords are obvious solutions, but both require resources on a continuous basis to achieve. Asking if this vast traffic might be an alternative led to many new ideas about value that could be developed for our members.

On the front, public facing side

IDEA 1: Build awareness.

Create awareness for your members and what they do to a much bigger audience than they can do on most of their own websites.

It is not easy for a small business to cost effectively market themselves and get traffic to their own websites. However, their non-profit has the power to attract a lot of traffic to their website through search and point that traffic already interested in what your members do at their content!

That is a powerful value for your members.

Using Google Analytics, it promoted how much traffic was visiting the website quarterly to start to sensitize the membership and other site visitors to the fact that this traffic was substantial and far, far greater than just the members. That is a common misperception that must be addressed among members.

MEMBERSHIP+13%   1560 MEMBERS
REVENUE +12% ᴈ **2014 RESULTS**
STUDENTS +24%
NEW VISITORS 55.4%
1,547,000 PAGES READ YTD ON SEGD.org
323 BIO'S CHAPTER EVENTS +24%
XLAB REGISTRATIONS 1209
+74.5% WEB VISITS 245,941
24 CHAPTERS
VIDEO'S 55 PAGE READS +76.8%
NEW ARTICLES 3648
CEO UPDATE

IDEA 2: A source of traffic for your members.

Become a source of traffic to their sites and potential leads and employees for their businesses.

Connecting the visitors coming to the non-profit site through to your member's websites as potentially interested customers (leads) would be new member value you are creating for your members from your website!

Insight two.

This was another ah-ha moment, realizing that to do this, we needed to make the most of the content on the website about **the members, their firms, projects and thought leadership.** I cannot stress enough how powerful a pivot this caused in the design of the website and thinking within staff about what the website can do for ALL members.

It changed EVERYTHING about how we thought.

The focus became extremely clear. The website would not be about the non-profit and in so doing we would have to rethink the website as a platform built completely around promoting and supporting the members!

Isn't that how it really should be? I know that a non-profit is not the staff or buildings or procedures, but rather it is the members!

Talking about a platform for the members immediately changed the conversation about the website and moved it away from where it had been stuck for so long as an electronic brochure, store and newsletter. I.e. what would a platform for our members look like? What could it do for them? What did they need? They were off and running now!

What kind of content should we create about our members?

The good this could do for the community immediately became clear when I realized that even as the CEO, I did not know what even a small percentage of our membership looked like! For the most part, they were invisible numbers. Not what I wanted with the reputation of being the friendliest, most helpful design non-profit!

IDEA 3: People.

Create a Member Bio with a headshot for every member to make the members visible for the community.

Create awareness for who they were on the site. These images would also serve to connect to search traffic for these members.

What's good for the goose is...

IDEA 4: Firms.

Create a similar profile page for firms. IT works the same way as for people

It was around this time that the reality of a few thousand bios on the site started to become a reality.

Members
2,288/335/191
Bios/Videos/Blogs

Firms
369/1,461
Listings/News

Projects
809/657
Awards/Features

HUNT
DESIGN

National Mall Wayfinding

Wayne Hunt, Principal

How might we connect them to the traffic flowing through the site and on the internet?

This developed over about a year as we slowly realized all the opportunities that were available to a member. Starting with Search Engine Optimization using the simple basic rules of SEO we were able to push the majority of the members Bios well up the Google Ranks onto the first page results for anyone searching for them due to Drupal's superior search friendly architecture. That took care of pulling external traffic to the site as well as providing in most cases members with the service of having the most informative solid article about them on the internet! That was a surprise to me how it could deliver such good content as part of a day job! The reason though was because of IDEA 5 below.

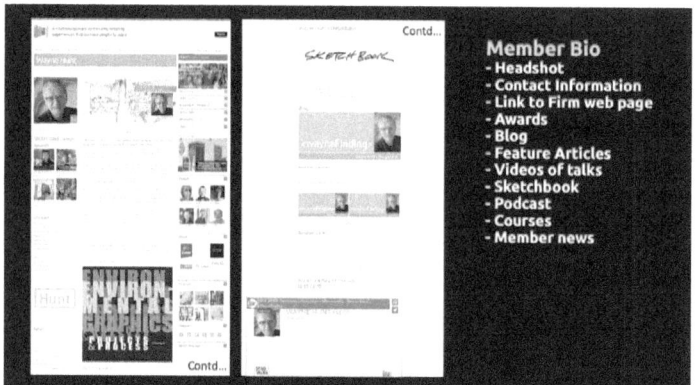

IDEA 5: Rich content.

Enriched Member Bios and Firm Listings.

Because all data; content, contact, firms awards etc. is contained in a single database, it was easy to create Member Bios that would gather everything ever published about a member along with their resume from award articles to Features, Member News, their Firm Logos and link to Videos of all the presentations they have given at our events, Sketchbooks, Blog articles, contact information from the AMS, Leadership/volunteer positions served with the non-profit and related tags to produce a complete picture of a members involvement with the organization. So much so that these pages i soon realized represented the best overview of a member available on the web! They are visually rich and with the videos embedded, they are also very compelling.

The same curating of content was done for Firms as well. The only thing I shied away from was adding the headshots with links to every member of a firm which was easily done. Why? Poaching!

IDEA 6: Promotion.

Add a Bio block and Firm block with 6 images each per page on every page of the site, maximizing the number of times they would be seen!

Though this did not seem like much at first when we calculated it, I realized that it had created a huge value. Member's images would be seen 18 million times (impressions) a year on the website's pages! The same applied to Firms and Projects.

This translated into providing each member with at least 10,000 impressions of their headshot a year and about 1,000 views of the Bio's from visitors clicking on them.

In Google Adword terms that's about $180 worth of pay per click referrals at Googles lowest average cost. This already represents nearly half the price of membership to SEGD. Imagine being able to create half the membership value, measurably with just the clicks! Quite some digital value for members already – and this to an interested, targeted audience.

If the member is known or their name is popular, they could be receiving benefits way more than your membership cost

117

already because of the size of your website, you will most likely be able to get much better search rankings for their names then their own much smaller websites will!

A word of caution. Of course, when you have members from a fortune 500 company, the likelihood is that you will not be able to compete with their own corporation's search, but you will even in those cases be surprised how effective you can be.

IDEA 7: Driving traffic to members sites.

Create links from member Bio's and Firm Listings to member firm sites.

By doing this the non-profit website acts like Google, delivering targeted traffic to member's sites. SEGD passed 50,000 of the 320,000 annual visitors along to the member's sites. Roughly 15%. Roughly $25,000 worth of referrals (outbound links in Google Analytics) in Google Adword terms. Not a huge amount, but another $20 of digital value for members that did not exist before.

Insight three.

With all the content now contained in a single database, I started to see the power of that to group it/ filter it and create slices of it for specific audiences internal as well as external!

How might we use the filters to add value for members and the greater community?

Some of the things were obvious, but the benefits were not.

IDEA 8: Recognizing participation.

Use the member's contributed value to the organization as one of the criteria in site search so that those who have been members for long and or have contributed generously in sponsorship or other ways come up higher in search results.

IDEA 9: Projects.

Use Tags to create search options for the Awards galleries.

 It is always surprising to visit a non-profit website and not find the actual work of award winners. Many non-profits seem to only list the names of the winners. However, on SEGD.org the Awards galleries are the most popular destination for visitors with about 36% of all traffic going to the Awards galleries every year. Creating a robust Awards experience for visitors is vital. Everyone wants recognition, especially from their peers, make sure the experience is special.

IDEA 10: Customization.

Filtering content. As a diverse profession, one of the challenges members face is being able to see/access just that part of the non-profit that is meaningful to them.

Filtering content seemed to be the ideal way to achieve select content for each niche or practice area. That very quickly lead me to understand that people have a need to see different selections of our information in a variety of different ways depending on what they are looking for, what vertical they practice in and what aspect of the profession most interests them.

The solution was to build landing pages for each of these filter criteria. The result was a staggering 55% increase in visitors and a doubling in page reads per visitor to 5 pages on average!

Equally as interesting was the 40% increase in search traffic over that period as the new URL's and Tags were indexed by Google. Percentages are one thing, pages read from people coming from search are quite another. That 40% increase translated to another 360,000 pages read a year in 2016.

120

This meant exposing our members, their firms and projects to another 60-80,000 visitors a year! Great exposure at no extra cost to the member! Try doing that with an expensive to produce magazine that costs you incrementally more per additional copy you print. This is of course the beauty of the web, it scales cheaply and associations need effective ways to scale.

The Xplore index was created to parse the content of SEGD into a matrix of Practice areas (the segments of the profession) and Industry Verticals (markets). Clicking on a category on the left produces an overview of all types of content produced by SEGD from Members Bios to Firms, Awards, Feature Articles, News, Thoughts from member's blog contributions to courses, events and videos from past events. This view is like the top of a "T". Click any of the more buttons and you get a page that digs deep down into any one of the content types like Features, Blogs, Awards or People.

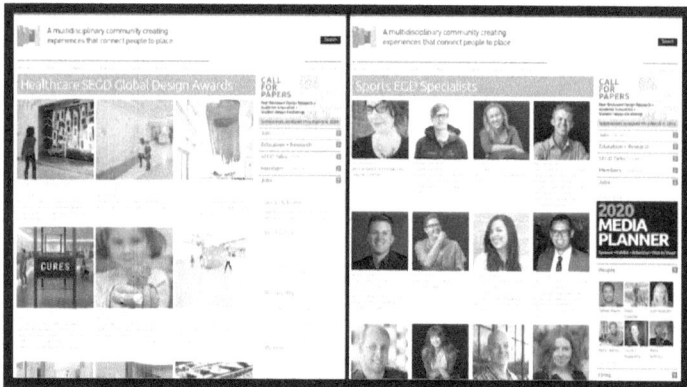

Insight four.

Geography matters! At least for many people. A National non-profit can quickly look just like that. National level activities, information, hero's and attention for only a few.

How might we enhance the website for local areas and make the content more meaningful for someone in one part of the country?

IDEA 11: Highlight chapter activities globally.

Integrate pages for all the chapters with their own admin permissions so that they have their own content pages to promote their events write blog posts about local news and activities.

From the non-profit perspective, the big advantage is that the entire membership finally understands a real sense of how many events are going on and how much happens in a year. They see what all the chapters were doing on the national site. It was hard to get going at first, but soon the Chapter Chairs started to see what each other were doing and the natural competitive nature of leaders started to kick in. The number of events went up and the effort and inventiveness of the events increased. Everyone benefited. So too did the number of requests to form new Chapters! SEGD went from 9 to 42 chapters in that time.

IDEA 12: Filter content by geography.

Filter the content by City, thus producing a slice of all the non-profits content for each chapter.

As you progress down the road of digital value creation the greater the need to customize will become. This is where Corporations are today, at the stage of trying to customize the entire visit experience for individual visitors to their sites to maximize their relevance to each customer.

This level of marketing customization is a very, very long way from where 95% of all non-profits are today so beware, we are being out paced in marketing terms! These types of web content management systems will cost you upwards of a million dollars to configure and then a lot more to develop thereafter. I believe unless non-profits develop their own systems on open source software, there is no chance of the non-profit world catching up or competing with that sort of investment in digital. See the Chapter on collaboration later in the book.

For now, there are still a lot of clever things like geographical tagging that can be implemented, and that will already get us all part of the way towards customization and a lot further down the road to customization than we currently are today.

Insight five.

Due to the way that the non-profit world has developed, the AMS function has been addressed through a few legacy systems designed and built specifically for the non-profit world. They have become web based, but what data is stored in them is not in your control. Realizing this, I understood that if I could integrate the AMS function into our website, that we could use the data to enrich and add to many other pieces of content. Imagine that whatever bits of information you have in your AMS visible only to staff could be make available for members as well. There is huge value in already gathered data you can unlock for the members, and the public if desired.

On the left, a member's Bio for the public with no contact information visible. On the right, the contact information visible and seamlessly integrated into the content of a member's bio. This is a much more elegant way to read about and find out information about a member than going through the member directory!

Insight 6

This took a lot longer to sink in, but when I really grasped the reality that the non-profit members visiting the website still only made up 0.3% of the unique traffic to the site a year, that I had to consider our audience as the greater community, not just the non-profit members. In my mind, the members were mentally starting to become the benefactors of whatever good work featured on the site and indeed this has been the case as the focus has shifted to asking what we need to do with/for the 99% of the traffic to add more value for our members and their firms.

IDEA 13: Member-only access Toolbox.

Create a suite of tools for members to help them find data for research and doing their jobs easier.

Create a member toolbox interface gathering all the vital resources a member needs to make business decisions, create proposals, do research at the front end of projects, gain access to bylaws and legal documentation easily.

A content portal offers access to a huge repository of data. If a non-profit has done its job of digitizing all its content right, it will be the repository of thousands of pages of information. This content is easily linked to traffic on the web through effective search optimization, but for that 0.4% of visitors who are your members, they struggle to find what they need by simply going to the website and hunting around. For this reason, I saw the need to build search tools that could deliver answers to specific questions that members encounter in their daily operations and in that way, it could become a more vital (yes, relevant!) resource for them.

The idea of a toolbox is not necessarily new, but a single page that gathers all the vital information for a professional to use to do their jobs is unique and was highly appreciated.

The toolbox is visible to the public, but when you click to access the tools as a non-member, it encourages you to join, acting as a huge advert for the value of membership!

IDEA 14: Rich content member directory.

A new much richer member directory

A good example of this was the combination of the back-end member directory with the content side of the website. The new member directory integrates headshots of the members and logos of their firms that link directly to these articles so if you are searching for someone to help you in a certain city, you can easily find them in the directory and in a single click read their bio or view the work of their firms.

IDEA 15: Image search.

An image search tool

Another example is that all members do research at the beginning of a design project looking for images of the type of work they are about to undertake and inspiration that they will paste onto a Pinterest board to create what is called a mood board.

These are used to give a client a frame of reference and the internal team a source of ideas. Pinterest is the social media platform of choice for doing this type of work, but on the front end of that, gathering the images can still be a time-consuming activity. You could build a filter for over 10,000 images to get them closer to what they were looking for and a direct link button to post these images on their Pinterest boards.

On the back end this involved adding tags to all the images so that they could be sorted by design and manufacturing criteria. Adding this sort of data to each image greatly enriches the value of the images as well as enhancing their search Optimization (SEO) on the web as they now exist as images with keywords!

On the back-administration end

IDEA 16: Visually rich data.

Add the headshots and firm logos to the AMS/CRM.

No big deal, except that now every staff member could see every member. That was a HUGE deal. At least 30-50% of your members are not known to the staff, maybe more, so actually seeing who you are talking to put a face to a name when staff interacted with them, they recognized a lot more people at conferences and events! The effect was huge! I should have guessed something was different when after the first week something went wrong and the whole staff were up in arms because the headshots had disappeared!

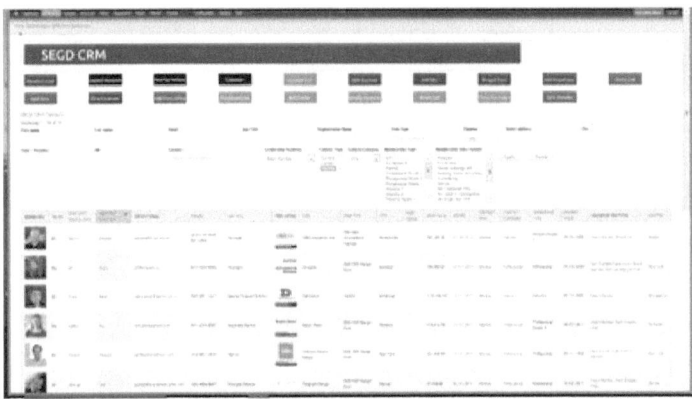

IDEA 17: Recognize member contributions and loyalty.

Membership value/engagement

Integrated into the administrative views are the total $ a member has spent with the non-profit and a listing of their volunteer positions so that on a phone call/search, it is very visible and easy for the staff to get a good sense of who they

129

are talking to and what value they have contributed to the organization at a glance.

The member's dashboard page ties everything available on a member into a single summary page. You can see others who work in their firm, ow much they spent this year, how long they have been members... it's all there.

As with any AMS, anything that can be done to make your staff's contact with a member more personal, customized and relevant will help to enable the staff to offer better customer service outreach and or problem solving for members which leads to higher satisfaction and hopefully engagement.

IDEA 18: Transparency.

Making everyone aware of how we are doing

Yet another huge advantage of the full integration of all non-profit data and back end functions is that it was easy to produce an integrated dashboard for the staff. Everyone works on the website every day in some form or other producing content, managing sales, servicing membership or promoting events.

IDEA 19: Segmentation for firms.

When I started this project, I had very little information on the members. Names, sometimes an e-mail (but not consistently), a phone number, firm name and address (Though never clear if these were the firms contact details or the members home details. It took about 2 years' work into categorizing all the firms the members belonged to in order to create a real profile of what the profession looked like for the membership. This included website links, a type classification, addresses to create a solid Geo tagging possibility for us, for instance associating firms with the Chapter pages so that it was possible to help visitors to find firms in their area easily – especially of they were members.

On the back end, it was amazing to see how within a few months this completely revolutionized our segmentation of communications for membership, awards and event registrations.

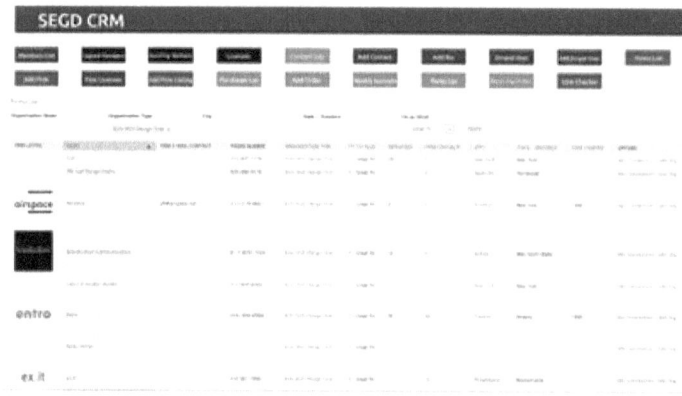

IDEA 20: Content Dashboards.

Content Dashboard

Tracking the content we were creating and the popularity of that content plus the number of reads helped us learn what was working for our members.

NOTE: Many images in this chapter are blurry to keep member details unreadable.

Chapter 7

Culture change: Conditions for success

A commitment to build creative competences in house.

It is easy to ask someone else to build you a new website. In fact, your best option to get started would be to hand them this book or go to the SEGD.org site and ask them to copy it. It works fantastically has generated amazing new value for the non-profit and you can save yourself 2 years' development if you do.

The learning is free, but you still have to do a ton of work to build your site. The goal is to move non-profits to the next level of value generation and to turn on thousands of creative engines across the non-profit world so that they can start to accelerate to the level of innovation of modern non-profits and associations. You're not a threat to SEGD because they have a creative engine running and they are in a rapid innovation mode already, so unless you do that as well, you would always be running behind where they are with their constant service upgrades and benefits improvements every month or quarter.

If you stop at the point of copying the latest version of their website or non-profit 2.0, you are completely missing the point of this book. That point being the reason that non-profits have not generated new value and continued to develop their relevance for their members is that in general they lack the core skills and competences on their staff that modern corporations need to create new products and services. Non-profits need coders, designers, developers and product managers in a team in-house to become real value generators! No great organization has got to where it is by outsourcing the core creation of their product or service!

Decide who owns service innovation.

Before you embark on a new website, you need to appoint a real product owner. This is not just a project owner internally who is not just shuffling budget between you and a vendor, but rather a tinkerer and creative who wants to build stuff and get under the hood of your website and understand the technologies that make it work and feels comfortable (over time) messing with it and changing it and improving it on a continuous basis.

At the beginning of this book I mentioned that you might try to get this from within your existing staff, but that most likely you will not be able to. I have yet to meet non-profit professionals who have anything near the right skills and competences to think in the above way or are even willing to or sufficiently confident enough to take HUGE risks. Do any of your staff have the deep desire to produce excellence and continuously beat the best out there? This is the sort of culture that you need to develop in your staff. It is most likely better to do this by bringing in this competence to seed the culture change. It will be a lot faster and cheaper in the end! These types of creatives are expensive as compared to non-profit salaries, but then the value they create is infinitely larger than their cost so you will be making a good investment by going down this path because most good creatives will solve real problems for you and advance your non-profit. Secondly, they will likely cost a lot less than the cost of using a vendor to build you a new site, so for the same cost you should be able to buy such a headcount for a few years. Now imagine what you can achieve with such a resource on tap everyday instead of just doing an initial build in a few months and then nothing for a few years!

Content Creation.

Content creation will become central to your staffs' functions in a way that it probably has not been before. Gone are the days of a publications staff working in isolation from the membership and the events teams!

The goal should be that everyone works on the website and everyone contributes to creating relevant new content. For a content model to work, it is necessary to break the old model of an editor and writer working on a publication alone. All staff need to contribute, including the leader to generate content fast enough to become a real content portal. Don't expect members to contribute bios, firm profiles or much of anything else. It is going to be up to you to create all the initial content. Members have a strong bias that whatever they do will be of a lot more value if they do it on the big social platforms like Facebook, Twitter and LinkedIn. Your staff will be the initial content contributors. Generating a bio for each member and search optimizing it is time consuming, but it adds a lot of value for the non-profit and the members.

Life is about to change in your non-profit with this new creative engine. Staff are going to have to scramble at first to keep up, but the good news is that innovation and creativity are infectious and before long everyone will pick up their work tempo as the energy levels get more animated! If you are lucky 7-hour workdays will fade as they did for the rest of the world who took on the digital value generation challenge almost 2 decades ago!

It's exciting, much higher risk in some ways and a lot of fun. Get ready for the ride!

Well, about that risk. Personally, I believe it is a lot lower risk than not changing your competences and ways of working, or worse still not grasping the concept of digital value creation.

Chapter 8

Measuring progress and defining success

What is not measured is not done. On the other hand, when you realize that you can measure everything, there is a strong tendency to measure, measure, measure without really producing any value from the results. Therefore, it is important to spend time thinking about what you are trying to achieve and what you need to measure to ensure that you are making steady progress towards achieving that goal because whatever it is, it is most likely measurable on the web.

In the case of SEGD, i wanted to measure if we were moving the bar from a non-profit being something that you should support to becoming vital for a professional's career and business development.

To do this, I had to measure:

1. How often people looked at members Bios, Firm Listings and projects to be able to communicate their effectiveness to member
2. Measure how many referral links were being sent to their websites
3. Who was looking at their content? The assumption of members is that it is just students, not potential clients
4. How often were the toolbox tools were being used
5. Overall traffic and page reads and demographics

Here are a few of the criteria you can easily measure which will give you a basic understanding of how your WEBSITE is performing.

Criteria:

- Traffic growth
- Visitor growth
- Page reads
- Time on page
- Registrations/purchases/memberships.
- Sentiment

Tools to help you measure:

- Google Analytics
- Leadfeeder
- Google Keyword Tool
- Google Webmaster's tools
- Internal counters and reports

What I am proposing in this book is that YOU can create value for your members. A decent goal would be to see if you can create 50% of your membership value digitally as a good starting point. Who would not say yes to doubling your member value?

Value should be measured by the members, not by the staff to understand what members really value. The principal is simple, but we very quickly discovered that members have little idea of the value of things digitally.

For the first pass, I evaluated the member value internally and then divided it by 10 to come to a "realistic" appraisal. However, the first round was in fact based on real alternatives and as such is a real indicator of value, if not the members own estimate!

SEGD's Digital Value for Members

The first pass looked like this:

SEGD's Digital Benefits		
Member Benefits	Views/year	***Value/ member/year
Be seen by visitors to SEGD.org interested in EGD	400,000	$150
Be seen by Potential Clients (firms visiting SEGDorg)	40,000	$75
Create awareness with Member Bios	500-1000	$200
Professional Development: educate yourself with 300+ SEGD Talks Videos	80,000+	$2,870
Generate interest from SEGD's Google search traffic	235,000	$50
Receive highly qualified traffic through outbound links*	100,000	$75
Create awareness with Firm Listings**	1000-2000	$800
SEGD Digital Benefits		$4,220

* Outbound links are referrals (people clicking on your linkedin/website link) from SEGD.org
** Firm Listings cost $500, but deliver $1,000-2,000 in comparable Google Adwords clicks
*** Estimates based on equivalent cost of buying Google adwords to achieve the same result on your own website

The goal was to create an additional 50% membership value digitally. No matter which way you look at it, arriving at 50% of the $375 membership dues is not difficult to do! The digital value created has far exceeded the membership cost already. And that is before trying to measure things like the effectiveness of the site as a search tool after you have done all the work of tagging, indexing and publishing great content! How about:

- The value of your non-profit putting a face to a name.
  - Many people join and never become active as we know, with these types of digital assets, they become at least part of the virtual community
- The understanding of the community that they come first.
- The increase in the value of belonging to your community for international members and those in geographic areas where it is difficult to participate in Chapter events is enormous. In fact, it becomes a strong reason to join.
- The ease of finding people/firms inspiration?

- Single sign on, seeing all your account information in one place?
- Getting information about your members into the top 5-10 (page 1) places of a google search?

There are many ways that your digital platform is benefitting your members at are difficult to measure, but they are there nevertheless.

Google Analytics

Google Analytics is a fantastic free tool from Google to measure what is happening on your website. Google analytics is a web traffic measurement tool, not a component of your customer relationship Management (CRM). It tells you about flows and the bigger picture.

There are many good tutorials (link) on the web for free to help you learn how to use Google Analytics.

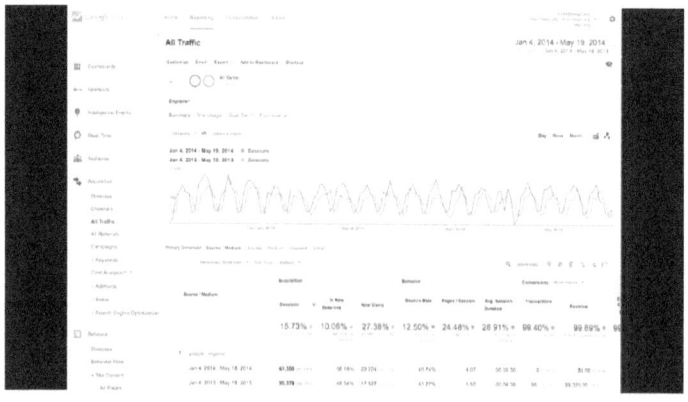

Leadfeeder

To manage relationships, learn user behavior and understand exactly who is visiting your site, you need to implement something like Leadfeeder, which is a very affordable (though somewhat limited) marketing tool to get closer to your customers. Leadfeeder will tell you from which companies your traffic is coming, often who that visitor is, if they are part of your mailing lists or linked in Contacts and what pages they visited in their visit so that you can gain an understanding of what their purpose was on your site. This is also how you will be able to build up use cases for your website. Leadfeeder, as the name suggests, can also directly tell you who to call to try to close deals in certain circumstances, i.e. when you see people go into your store, place a membership registration into their shopping cart, but then abandon the sale. They are very, very close to becoming a member and s personal call, might really help to close that deal.

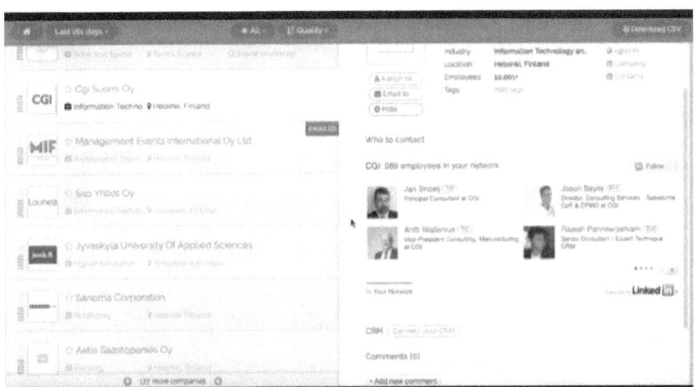

Google Keyword Tool

The Google keyword tool is useful to determine how many people are searching for certain key words a month and therefore to help you build up a picture of how well you are doing at Keyword search optimization. On any Google search page, you can see how many places Google found with the search terms (how much information has been produced about that keyword term) Many people confuse that with how many people are looking for that information! Having a sense of both gives you a sense of the competition to find people looking for the keyword term and therefore your likelihood of succeeding at getting that traffic.

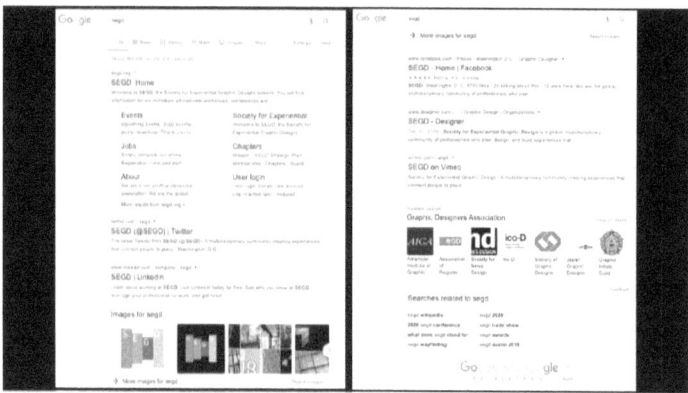

277,000 results were found for the search term "SEGD", but the number of monthly searches for the term were only between 1-10,000. This demonstrates the difference between the amount of information Google has indexed and the number of people searching for that information!

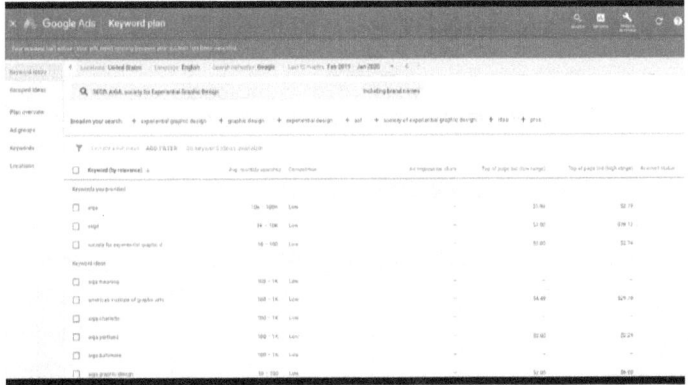

Google Webmaster tools

Google Webmaster tools helps you see details about how your site appears for search, who connects to your site and any problems the search engines are seeing. It also gives a list of search terms and the traffic coming from each of those terms to your site.

Internal Dashboards

There are probably several performance measurements that you make internally as a non-profit such as average sales, membership numbers, attendance at events, sales growth etc. With a completely integrated system many of these can be created and accessible to all admins logged in.

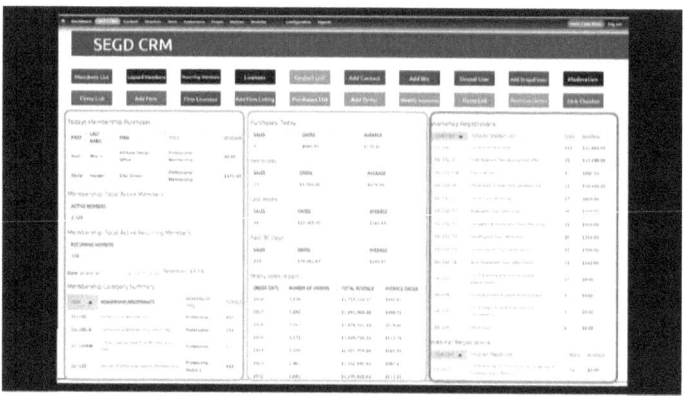

Chapter 9

The case for collaboration

Non-profits have a scale problem that can be overcome through a new model of collaboration

Scale is what the digital age is all about. As non-profits, we are excluded from being able to scale in the way that most web companies are because we serve specific industries, professions and target audiences.

In marketing terms this is most often seen as a big plus to have a clearly defined target audience, however in web terms it is not as scale is what brings revenues and the ability to apply the sort of resources you need to constantly improve a platform such as Google or Facebook.

On the plus side a non-profit has scale that few of its members have, so FOR THE MEMBERSHIP, an Non-profits scale should be an asset and can be as we have described in this book.

Here's a novel thought about ways to use scale.

Imagine if a group of non-profits collaborated on creating a high-quality web platform for all to share.

There are three compelling reasons to collaborate.

1. It's the only way that "the non-profit world" can compete against venture backed internet competitors!
2. If they pooled resources to develop this platform and constantly evolved it for the common good of their

members, the collective would be able to create a far more sophisticated platform than any one of them going it alone. Non-profits audiences have similar needs, with specific differences, but the differences can probably be dealt with at the configuration level as opposed to the platform, architecture or code level.

3. All professions would benefit from being linked to the professions/target groups who need their services. In other words, their customers and as standalone organizations, their audiences are the members, far less so the customers of the members. Creating a common platform would allow for customers to be connected to professions!

This approach should not be confused with the present vendor captive client model which is completely different and far from being user centric, responsive or efficient for the clients. In a collaborative model, it is the users' needs that drive the development of the platform, not the vendor's business model!

Building websites that do more than act as an electronic brochure is becoming very expensive as the sites become functional machines versus just digital pages. The price of an advanced website now exceeds what most Non-profits can afford, putting them in the unfortunate position of slipping further behind their corporate competitors. Something must change in how we approach digital services and how we create digital value if non-profits are to become competitive.

The first stop along this road is to create an internal creative services development team. The second is probably some sort of cross non-profit model to leverage scarce creation competences and resources. Within Drupal, it is already possible to share the basic code for websites amongst many sites and still customize a layer on top of that basic code.

Collaboration is a huge clue as to how non-profits could become truly competitive again.

Chapter 10

Conclusion

If you are thinking differently about your non-profit and its digital presence at this point, this book has achieved its goal.

Perhaps a good measure of what you might expect would be to provide some results from the SEGD example as a benchmark. Every non-profit is different, but hopefully this is a reasonable point to start as it is a small non-profit and the hope is that all bigger on-profits can expect even better results.

Benchmark.

From January 2013 to December 2016. A three-year timeframe.

SEGD Web Metrics 2013-2016			
Metric	**2013**	**2016**	**% Improvement**
Visits	181,583	474,178	161%
Visitors	106,601	319,852	200%
New Visitors	103,749	311,675	200%
Pageviews	932,456	3,640,470	290%
Pages/session	5	7.68	49%
New Sessions	56%	67%	18%
Annual Revenue	1,440,549	1,851,702	29%
Annual Members	1,456	1,830	26%
Content	3,500	5,689	63%

Member Satisfaction.

While the numbers speak loud and clear, it is the unspoken that speaks louder. In 2013, we heard a lot from members that they were not renewing because they did not find value in membership. By the end of 2016, we did not hear that complaint and in fact the number of people not renewing a year had reduced as more member content and member tools became available and while not accessible, they were made publicly visible as teasers to potential members!

Here is a checklist of the ideas in the book that you can return to often to remind yourself of your options and why you are taking this journey.

Reasons to become more like for-profit corporations.

1. They are value creation machines. Non-profits need to adopt the value creation functions, but then with heart!
2. The internet is a tool that all organizations can use to create value for customers, not just for-profit corporations.
3. Corporations have teams with creative competences that drive innovation that non-profits desperately need to develop to complement their excellent administrative staff.

Non-profits need a change in the type of skills they have on the staff team to accelerate the rate at which they create useful value for their members. In most corporation's products/services are refreshed/replaced from every few weeks as in fashion design to every few years for much larger capital-intensive products like cars, but they are all replaced with upgrades often! With internet companies, the upgrade process is practically continuous.

At an individual non-profit level, shifting from an old-style non-profit is big and will create real new value for the non-profit's membership that far exceed where the non-profits magazine or other publications can take you.

In our SEGD example we were able to prove that the digital value created per member was worth more than 3.5 times the cost of membership per year. Try doing that with physical programs and add on's.

Finally, here's a thought to leave you with.

Imagine of all non-profits adopted a digital forward approach. If all non-profits were making this sort of progress digitally, the non-profit sector of the economy could potentially become huge value creation engines for the world!

But wait! Is that not what we are supposed to be doing? Is that not the reason non-profits exist?

References

1. Race for Relevance: Harris Coerver and Mary Byers
2. Stanford d.school:
   https://dschool.stanford.edu/resources/the-bootcamp-bootleg
3. Nielsen Norman Group:
   https://www.nngroup.com/articles/top-10-enduring/

Appendix 1: Drupal Modules for a non-profit 2.0 website

Drupal 7 modules needed to create the functionality discussed in this book. If you need help e-mail clivero@gmail.com **to get you set up.**

1. Chaos Tools
2. Administration Menu
3. Administration Views
4. Advanced Queues
5. Views
6. Panels
7. Font your face (Google Ubuntu font)
8. Address Field
9. Apps Compatible
10. Authorize.Net (or other credit card processing service)
11. Backup and Migrate
12. Bean
13. Better Exposed Filters
14. BlueOI External Payment (Recurring Payments?)
15. Calendar
16. CAPTCHA
17. CAPTCHA Riddler
18. Commerce
19. Commerce Google Analytics
20. Charts
21. Chosen
22. Cloudflare

53. Global redirect
54. Google Analytics Push
55. Google Analytics
56. Google Charts
57. Google Font API
58. Google webfont Loader API
59. Help
60. Highcharts
61. Image Link Formatter
62. Image Maximum Size Crop
63. Inline Conditions
64. Inline Entity Form (Core?)
65. jCarousel
66. jQuery Update
67. Link Checker
68. Link
69. Login Toboggan (Rules integration and content access integration? Part of Login Toboggan?)
70. Masonary API
71. Masonary Views
72. Media Browser Plus
73. Media Internet sources/WYSIWYG View Mode (part of Media Browser?)
74. Media
75. Menu (Attributes/token? Part of?)
76. Message Notify
77. Message
78. Metatag (part of Core?)
79. Metatag Dublin Core
80. Metatag Panels
81. Metatag Views
82. Mime Mail Action
83. Mime Mail CSS Compressor
84. Mime Mail

www.ingramcontent.com/pod-product-compliance
Lightning Source LLC
Chambersburg PA
CBHW021415210526
45463CB00001B/380